SOUTH LA

AN AFROCENTRIC CITY GUIDE TO SOUTH LOS ANGELES

First Printing 2023

ISBN 978-1-7361888-5-9 (paperback)
ISBN 978-1-7361888-6-6 (ebook)

Published by Go Crenshaw Publications
The Crenshaw District, Los Angeles, CA
www.gocrenshaw.com | www.gocrenshaw.shop

DR. RANDAL HENRY

GO CRENSHAW

The Crenshaw District, Los Angeles, CA

DEDICATION

Go South LA is dedicated to the people of South Los Angeles, California.

CONTENTS

INTRODUCTION

There is no other city guide like *Go South LA*, the afrocentric city guide to over 700 things that you can see, do, hear, taste and experience in and around South Los Angeles, California. *Go South LA* features 225 distinct activity categories, organized alphabetically and by distance, listing hundreds of interesting things that can be found in (or nearby) South LA. Written from the perspective of someone who was born, raised and lives in South Los Angeles, Go South LA fills an important niche for local residents, visitors from other parts of California, out-of-state guests, and tourists from around the globe who want to learn more about Black South LA and how it is interconnected with other parts of the city.

In *Go South LA* you'll find everything from Adobes, Airports and Architecture; Books, Bars and Bar-B Que; Leimert Park, Destination Crenshaw and Nipsey Hussle Square; Parks, Pools and Golf Courses; the Taste of Soul Festival, Soul Food and Creole/ Cajun Cuisine; the Watts Towers, Wine and Wetlands; Mexican Excursions and, Malcolm X's, Martin Luther King Jr and Biddy Mason Commemoration Sites. If you are interested in a city guide that features South LA's history, food, recreation, entertainment and services, from a Pan-African/Black perspective, you will find this guide invaluable.

ABOUT SOUTH LOS ANGELES

Home to one of the largest concentrations of African Americans, Caribbean Americans and LatinX Americans in the United States, South LA is world-famous for civil rights advocacy, jazz, soul, dance, multiculturalism, creativity, dynamism, hip-hop royalty, afro-centricity and all kinds of things that you can learn more about by reading this city guide.

South Los Angeles, California (South LA) is a great place to live, work, play, go to school, exercise, take a walk, learn something

11

new, go hiking, see a sporting event, meditate, go dancing, buy something to wear, go to a museum or get something to eat.

Owing to its central location, South LA   is attracting more travelers and visitors. It's close to the Los Angeles International Airport, the beach, sports and entertainment centers like the Los Angeles Coliseum, Hollywood, LA Live and Sofi Stadium as well as major attractions like Universal Studios, Knott's Berry Farm and Disneyland.

With the renaissance of light rail bisecting the community and providing transportation from LA International Airport to DTLA to Hollywood to UCLA to the beach and back, South LA is at the center of it all - and is poised and polished to attract visitors, tourists and business leading up to, during and beyond the 2028 Olympic Games.

South LA has had world-wide influence on the way people dress, act, speak, sing, dance, rap, clown, play music, modify cars, tattoo, depict art, do sports, and understand diversity around the globe - basically South LA influences everything. Whether in the best of times or in the worst of times there is no place like South LA.

WHY DID I WRITE GO SOUTH LA?

Go South LA was conceived during a trip to Aswan, Egypt. I wished I had an afrocentric city guide that showed unabashed love for South LA like my Nubian guide Juma was showing for the city of Aswan, Egypt. I'd grown tired of hearing South LA - my home - described from the vantage of people who do not love it. I wanted to read a 'city guide' about South LA that expressed the deep love that the people of South Los Angeles - particularly African Americans - have for South LA. I noted that travel books and city guides from places in South America, Central America and Africa with social, economic, political and public health challenges equal to or greater than those of South LA, did not hesitate to talk about

12

all the cool things that you could see, do and experience in their cities. So I looked for one. My search led me to some cool websites like Black Cultural Events, Blackout Cinema, Soul of America and a very good book named the African American Travel Guide but, I didn't find anything specific to South Los Angeles, so I completed my research and wrote *Go South LA*.

HOW FAR IS IT FROM KING AND CRENSHAW?

Everything in *Go South LA* is measured in terms of its distance (i.e. miles) from Martin Luther King Jr (King) Blvd and Crenshaw Blvd, the geo-cultural center of South LA. More than 300 of them are within 5 miles of King and Crenshaw, 220 of them are within 5.1 miles to 10.0 miles, another 115 are 10.1 to 15 miles, over 60 from 15.1 to 30 miles, and about 30 from 30.1 miles or more.

Each location has been surveyed by distance from King Blvd x Crenshaw Blvd and assigned a corresponding 'pin'. Use the five color-coded 'pins' described below to assess distance when making travel plans. Refer to the Appendix for more information on travel distances.

Black Pins indicate locations from 0.0 miles to 5.0 miles from King and Crenshaw.

0.0

Red Pins indicate locations from 5.1 to 10.0 miles from King and Crenshaw.

5.1

Orange Pins indicate locations from 10.1 to 15 miles from King and Crenshaw.

10.1

Blue Pins indicate locations from 15.1 Miles to 30.0 Miles from King and Crenshaw.

15.1

Green Pins indicate locations from 30.1 miles and more from King and Crenshaw.

30.1

KNOW BEFORE YOU GO

Although much effort has been expended to ensure that the information included in this book is correct, many businesses (especially restaurants and comedy clubs) change their hours of operation, move or close. Before going to see, do, hear, taste or experience any of the locations included in this book, it's a good idea to do an internet search for:

- Hours of operation
- Prices/fees
- Parking information
- Directions
- Public transit options

SHARE YOUR EXPERIENCE ON INSTAGRAM OR FACEBOOK

Last, we love to know how you're using *Go South LA*. If you visit any of the places listed in this book, please leave a post on Instagram or Facebook. Don't forget to tag us @gocrenshaw and to include the hashtag #GoCrenshaw or #GoSouthLA in your posts. We'd love to hear from you.

FOLLOW US ON SOCIAL MEDIA

If you like the book or if want to learn more about the history and culture of South Los Angeles, follow us on Instagram at @gocrenshaw or on Facebook at Go Crenshaw. Visit our website at **www.gocrenshaw.com** to join our mailing list. Thank you.

700 THINGS TO SEE, DO, HEAR TASTE AND EXPERIENCE IN SOUTH LOS ANGELES LISTED FROM A TO Z:

A

ADOBES

Adobes, buildings made from mud bricks, wood and tar, are representative of LA's Spanish colonial period. See Historic Parks, Museums and Olvera Street for more information.

📍 **Avila Adobe**
7.7 *10 Olvera St, LA 90012.*
Built in 1818. California Historic Landmark #145.

📍 **Centinela Adobe**
5.5 *7634 Midfield Ave, LA 90045.*
Built in 1834.

📍 **Dominguez Rancho Adobe**
18.2 *18127 S. Alameda St. Compton 90220.*

📍 **Pio Pico Adobe**
23.7 *6003 Pioneer Boulevard, Whittier, 90606.*

📍 **Rancho Los Alamitos Adobe**
27.3 *6400 Bixby Hill Road, Long Beach 90815.*
Built in 1800.

📍 **Sanchez Ranch Adobe**
0.7 *3725 Don Felipe Dr., LA 90008.*
Built in 1790. LA Historic-Cultural Landmark #487.

AFRICAN MARKETS/MARKETPLACES

There are numerous places to find fashions, foods and culture. See Baldwin Hills Crenshaw Plaza, Caribbean Markets, Leimert Park, Farmers Markets, Markets, Market Street and Mercado or search "African Markets" for more information.

African Image
3.5
1878 S Western Ave, LA 90006.
Beauty supply by black women for black women.

African Marketplace and Drum Circle
0.5
43rd and Degnan, LA 90008.
Sundays 10am to 5pm.

Baba African Mini Mart
1.9
2063 W Jefferson Blvd, LA 90018.
African food, goods and clothes.

Kutula by Africana
1.5
4438 W Slauson Ave, LA 90043.
African fashion.

Minaco Ventures African Food Market
6.0
8606 ½ S Vermont Ave, LA 90044.
African food, goods and clothes.

Queen Aminah's
0.6
4339 Degnan Blvd, LA 90008.
Fashionable clothing.

Tropical Foods African Market
22.7 *4114 Orange Ave, Long Beach 90807.*

West LA International Market
10817 Venice blvd, LA 90034.
5.0 Halal foods and international groceries.

AIRPLANE PARK

Aviation Park
11022 Aviation Blvd, LA 90045.
7.0 Sixteen life-size fighter planes Children's playground.
Check out the Proud Bird Food Bazaar.

AIRPORTS

See Aviation Park and Aviation Themed Restaurants for more airplane-related information.

Compton Woodley Airport
901 W Alondra Blvd, Compton 90220.
13.4 Annual aviation fair, flight training, aeronautical museum, helicopter and plane rides.

Hawthorne Municipal Airport (HHR)
12101 Crenshaw Blvd, Hawthorne 90250.
6.5 General aviation aircraft. Flight training schools.

Hollywood Burbank Airport (BUR)
2627 N Hollywood Way, Burbank 91505.
14.2 Only LA airport with direct rail connection to DTLA.

John Wayne Airport (SNA)
43.3 Serves Orange County.

Long Beach Airport (LGB)
25.0 *4100 Donald Douglas Dr, Long Beach 90808.*
Serves Long Beach and South Bay.

Los Angeles International Airport (LAX)
7.3 *One World Way, LA, 90045.*
World's fifth-busiest airport.

McCarran International Airport (LAS)
272 *5757 Wayne Newton Blvd, Las Vegas, NV 89119.*

Ontario International Airport (ONT)
Ontario 91761.
47.5 Serves the Inland Empire.

San Gabriel Valley Airport (SGVA)
4233 Santa Anita Ave, El Monte, CA 91731.
22.0 Home to aircraft, a restaurant, and aviation-related businesses.

Santa Monica Airport (SMO)
3233 Donald Douglas Loop, Santa Monica 90405.
9.9 General aviation. Scheduled to close in 2028.

Tijuana International Airport
148 Tijuana, Mexico.

AMUSEMENT PARKS

Disney's California Adventure Park
32.9 *1313 Disneyland Dr, Anaheim 92802.*

Disneyland
32.9 *1313 Disneyland Dr, Anaheim 92802.*

Go Kart World

21830 Recreation Rd, Carson 90745.

16.9 Family amusement park. Recreational and competitive driving. All ages and skill levels.

Golf N' Stuff

10555 Firestone Blvd, Norwalk 90650.

19.8 18-hole mini-golf course, arcade, go-karts and rides.

Knott's Berry Farm

8039 Beach Blvd, Buena Park 90620.

28.1 Rides, shows, and attractions inspired by the history and culture of California.

MagIQ Escape Room

1446 S Robertson Blvd, LA 90035.

5.1 Live adventure, gaming and escapes.

Pan Pacific Park

380 Santa Monica Pier, Santa Monica 90401.

11.7 Rides, midway games, ocean front specialty food outlets and shopping.

Six Flags Magic Mountain

41.1 *26101 Magic Mountain Pkwy, Valencia 91355.*

Sky Zone Trampoline Park

1625 W 190th St, Gardena 90248.

16.9 Indoor trampoline park. Freestyle bouncing, dodgeball, and fitness programs.

Two Bit Circus

634 Mateo St, LA 90021.

8.9 Tech-infused Big Top. Interactive entertainment. Free entry. All ages welcome.

Universal Studios Hollywood

11.3 100 Universal City Plaza, Universal City 91608.
Film oriented theme park. Rides, dining, shopping, entertainment and seasonal events.

AQUATIC CENTERS

See Beaches, Lakes, Swimming Pools and Water Parks for more aquatic-related information.

Hansen Dam Aquatic Center

30.5 *11798 Foothill Blvd. Lake View Terrace 91342.*

UCLA Marina Aquatic Center

9.1 *14001 Fiji Way, Marina del Rey 90292.*

AQUARIUMS

See Beaches, Oceans, etc for more water-related information.

Aquarium of the Pacific

24.2 *100 Aquarium Way, Long Beach 90802.*

Cabrillo Marine Aquarium

25.2 *3720 Stephen M. White Dr, San Pedro 90731.*

California Science Center Kelp Forest

3.6 *700 Exposition Park Dr, LA 90037.*
Free.

Roundhouse Aquarium

13.4 *Manhattan Beach Pier, Manhattan Beach, 90266.*
Free.

Heal the Bay Aquarium

11.5　*1600 Ocean Front Walk, Santa Monica 90401.*

ARBORETUMS

Check out Gardens (i.e., Botanical, Chinese, and Japanese Gardens), Natural Parks, for more garden-related information.

Chavez Ravine Arboretum

7.9　*929 Academy Rd, LA 90012.*

Los Angeles County Arboretum

23.4　*301 N. Baldwin Ave, Arcadia, 91007.*

ARCHITECTURE

Angeles Funeral Home

3875 Crenshaw Blvd. LA 90008.

0.4　Designed by Paul R. Williams. Los Angeles Historic-Cultural Monument #774.

Angel's Flight Railway

350 S Grand Ave, LA 90071.

6.6　LA Historic-Cultural Landmark #4

Central Public Library

630 W 5th St, LA 90071.

7.2　Third largest central library in the U.S.

Dunbar Hotel

4225 S Central Ave, LA 90011.

4.8　Former focal point of LA's Black community. Los Angeles Historic-Cultural Monument #131.

Lincoln Theater Historic Site
5.9 *2300 S Central Ave, LA 90011.*
Hosted shows by Black entertainers during the segregation era. LA Historic-Cultural Landmark #744.

Los Angeles City Hall
7.0 *200 N Spring St, LA 90012*
LA Historic-Cultural Landmark #150.

Los Angeles Union Station
8.3 *800 N Alameda St, LA 90012.*

Orpheum Theater
6.8 *842 S Broadway, LA 90014.*
Art deco.

Saban Theater
5.5 *8440 Wilshire Blvd. Beverly Hills 90211.*
Art deco.

Shrine Auditorium
4.8 *665 W. Jefferson Blvd. LA 90007.*
LA Historic-Cultural Landmark #139.

Theme Building at LAX
7.6 *201 World Way, LA 90045.*
Designed by Paul R. Williams. LA Historic-Cultural Landmark #570.

Vision Theater
0.8 *3341 W 43rd Place, LA 90008.*

Watts Towers
12.8 *1727 E. 107th St. LA 90002.*
Designed and built by Simon Rodia. LA Historic-Cultural Landmark #15. CA Historical Landmark #993.

Watts Train Station

1686 E 103rd St, LA 90002.

10.5   LA Historic-Cultural Landmark #36.

What Wall (1998)

3524 Hayden Ave, Culver City 90232.

3.2   By Eric Moss for Culver City's Architecture as Art program.

The Wiltern Theater

3790 Wilshire Blvd. LA 90010.

4.4   Art Deco performing arts theater.

28th Street YMCA

2800-2812 Paloma St, LA 90011.

5.6   Designed by Paul R. Williams. LA Historic-Cultural Landmark #851.

ART

See Art Centers, Cultural Centers, Performing Arts, Photography, Public Art and Museums.

ART CENTERS

See also Cultural Centers for more Art Center related information.

Fernando Pullum Community Arts Center

3351 W. 43rd St., LA 90008.

0.7   Youth arts center.

📍 **La Plaza de Cultura y Artes**
6.2   *501 N. Main St., LA 90012.*

📍 **Torrance Cultural Arts Center**
13.9   *3330 Civic Center Dr, Torrance 90503.*

📍 **Watts Towers Arts Center**
10.5   *1727 E. 107th St. LA 90002.*

📍 **William Grant Still Arts Center — Designated Cultural Center**
2.1   *2520 S W View St, LA 90016.*

ART PARKS

See Arboretums, Museums and Sculpture Gardens for more art park-related information.

📍 **Barnsdall Art Park**
8.2   *4800 Hollywood Blvd, LA 90027.*
Art classes, museum, tours, theatre and festivals celebrating cultural diversity.

📍 **Grevillea Art Park**
4.7   *101 E Kelso St, Inglewood 90301.*
World's largest petrachrome mural.

ART WALKS

See Arboretums Museums and Walking Paths for more Walking and art walk-related information.

Downtown LA Art Walk
W 4th St, LA 90013.
7.5   Galleries, local murals and street art.

Downtown Long Beach Art Walk
501 E Broadway, Long Beah 90802.
24.4 Seven city blocks art in 5 galleries, 21 murals, and 30 businesses.

Leimert Park Art Walk
0.4   Last Sunday of the Month. 2pm to 8pm.

Venice Art Walk
10.1 Held in May. Features tours, music, food and art.

AVIATION THEMED RESTAURANTS

See Restaurants for more food, dining and restaurant-related options.

Proud Bird Food Bazaar and Event Center
11022 Aviation Blvd, LA 90045.
7.0   Views of LAX planes, interactive aviation exhibits and kid-friendly airplane park

Annia's Kitchen
4233 Santa Anita Ave, El Monte 91731.
22.0 Home to aircraft and Annia's Kitchen, a casual eatery serving Mexican & American fare in the lobby of the San Gabriel Valley Airport.

Skycap Cafe:
901 W Alondra Blvd, Compton 90220.
13.4 Located at Compton-Woodley Airport.

B

BAKERIES

📍 **Heavenly Cakes Creations**
1.5 *2916 W Vernon Ave, LA 90008.*

📍 **M'Dears Bakery & Bistro**
7717 S Western Ave, LA 90047.
4.2 Soul food and desserts.

📍 **Normandie French Bakery & Bistro**
2.6 *3022 S Cochran Ave, LA 90016.*

📍 **Shabazz Bakery**
446 S Market St #2310, Inglewood, 90301.
4.6 See Rosalie's Caribbean Cuisine.

📍 **Sweet E's Bake Shop**
1.8 *4574 W Adams Blvd, LA 90016.*

📍 **Southern Girl Bakery & Cafe**
0.2 *3650 W MLK Jr Blvd. LA 90008.*

BAR-B-QUE

See Restaurants for more food, dining and restaurant-related options.

📍 **Barbeque King**
3.7 *5309 Vermont Ave, LA 90037.*

Bludso's Bar & Que
6.6 *609 N La Brea Ave, LA 90036.*

Brother Bar-B-Que
3.0 *7725 Crenshaw Blvd, LA 90043.*

Hong Kong BBQ Restaurant
7.7 *803 N Broadway, LA 90012.*

Korean BBQ
6.8 *123 Onizuka St #302, LA 90012.*
In Weller Court.

Lucilles's Smokehouse
5.0 *6000 Sepulveda Blvd, Culver City 90230.*
Inside mall.

Phillips Bar-B-Que Take-Out Restaurant
Popular take-out spot. Two locations:

1.6 *2619 Crenshaw Blvd, LA 90016.*

4.1 *Centinela Ave, Inglewood 90302.*

Ray's Halal Texas BBQ
7.7 *6038 Santa Fe Ave, Huntington Park 90225.*

Spring Street Smokehouse Bar-B-Que
7.4 *640 N. Spring Street, LA 90012.*

The Wood Bar-B-Que and Sports Lounge
4.2 129 N Market St, Inglewood 90301.

Woody's Bar-B-Q:

📍 *475 S. Market St., Inglewood 90301.*
3.5

📍 *1958 W. Florence Ave, LA 90047.*
4.5

BARS

See Restaurants, Wine and Wineries for more information.

📍 **Harold and Belle's New Orleans Restaurant & Bar**
1.5   *2920 W. Jefferson Blvd, LA 90018.*

📍 **Hollywood Park Casino & Sports Bar**
5.5   *3883 W Century Blvd, Inglewood, 90303.*

📍 **La Louisianne Restaurant & Bar**
2.6   *5812 Overhill Dr, LA 90043.*

📍 **Lavender Blue Restaurant & Lounge**
       3310 W. Manchester Blvd, Inglewood, 90305.
3.9   Jazz, blues and food.

📍 **Old Man Spirit Bar**
7.4   *12517 W. Washington Blvd, LA 90066.*

📍 **Pips on La Brea**
       1356 S. La Brea Ave, LA 90019.
3.4   Restaurant. Bar. Wine. Live Jazz. Italian food.

📍 **Post and Beam**
       3767 Santa Rosalia Dr, LA 90008.
0.3   Restaurant. Bar. Patio. Frequent live jazz.

📍 **The Cork Bar and Grill**
1.9 *4771 W. Adams Blvd, LA 90016.*

📍 **The District Restaurant and Bar**
0.3 *3888 Crenshaw Blvd, LA 90008.*

📍 **The Nile Restaurant and Bar**
4.5 *207 S Market St, Inglewood 90301.*

BASKETBALL

See Bars, Colleges, Sports Lounges, Sports Stadiums, and Universities to find more basketball related information.

📍 **Drew League Basketball**
1601 E. 120th St. LA 90059.
11.5 Ballers, street legends and pro's.

📍 **Venice Basketball Courts**
9.4 *1708-1798 Ocean Front Walk, Venice, 90292.*

BEACHES

See Bike Paths, Historically Black Beaches, and Hiking Trails for more beach related information.

📍 **Bruce's Beach**
2600 Highland Ave, Manhattan Beach, 90266.
11.9 Historic site of African American beach resort.

📍 **Dockweiler Beach**
11.3 *12000 Vista Del Mar, Playa Del Rey 90293.*

Hermosa Beach

13.7 *Hermosa Beach 90254.*
Over 94 acres of public beach, excellent surf, good swimming areas and volleyball nets.

Lighthouse Beach

10.3 *4200 Ocean Front Walk, Marina Del Rey, 90292.*

Mother's Beach

9.0 *4135 Admiralty Way, Marina Del Rey 90292.*
Playground. Picnic tables. Kid-friendly. Surf-free sheltered beach.

Original Muscle Beach

12.0 *Ocean Front Walk, Santa Monica 90401.*

Playa Del Rey Beach

12.0 *7313-7351 S Marine Ave, PDR 90293.*

Redondo Beach Arcade, Fish Market, Fun Factory, Pier and Seaside Lagoon

14.0 *123 Intl. Boardwalk, Redondo Beach 90277.*
Panoramic ocean views. Harbor cruises. Whale watching.

Santa Monica State Beach

12.0 *Santa Monica 90401.*

The Inkwell

12.0 *Santa Monica 90401.*
Site of historic African American beach.

Venice Beach

10.0 *1800 Ocean Front Walk, Venice 90291.*
World famous Boardwalk, Muscle Beach and Pier.

Will Rogers State Beach

13.9 *17000 Pacific Coast Hwy, Pacific Palisades, 90272.*
Beach wheelchairs available.

Zuma Beach

31.8 *30000 Pacific Coast Highway, Malibu.*
Known for its long, wide sands and excellent surf.

BELIZEAN FOOD

See Restaurants for more options.

Little Belize
4.4 *17 E. Nutwood St, Inglewood 90301.*

Pepper's Jamaican Belizean Cuisine
2.5 *2166 W Slauson Ave, LA 90047.*

BEVERLY HILLS

See Cities and Neighborhoods for more information.

BIKE PATHS

See Arboretums, Art Walks, Beaches, Bike Paths, Walking Paths and Hiking Trails, etc,... for more information about walking paths and hiking trails.

Ballona Creek Bike Path
3.5 *Culver City 90232.*
Enter on Duquesne Ave near Jefferson Blvd.

Compton Creek Bike Path

Compton 90220.

11.5 Runs along the LA River from Compton to Carson.

Marvin Braude Bike Trail

15100 Ocean Front Walk, Pacific Palisades, 90272.

14.5 Runs from Will Rogers Beach to Torrance.

BIKE SHOPS

See Beaches, Hiking Trails, and Walking Paths for more information.

Linares Bike Shop

4.0 *4418 S Broadway, LA 90037.*

Primo's Bike Shop

2.2 *1645 W Vernon Ave, LA 90062.*

Ride On Bike Co-op

4319 Degnan Blvd, LA 90008.

0.6 Full service bicycle shop.

BISTROS

See Bakeries for more information.

BLUES MUSIC

Barbara Morrison Performing Arts Center

4305 Degnan Blvd, LA 90008.

0.6 Jazz and blues

◉ **Lavender Blue Restaurant Lounge**
3.9 *3310 W. Manchester Blvd., Inglewood, 90305.*
Live jazz and blues with delicious food.

Nothing But the Blues Radio Program
Broadcast Saturdays from 2:00 PM until 6:00 PM, and
Sunday from 2:00 PM until 7:00 PM PST. Hosted by
Gary Wagner on KJZZ radio station 88.1 FM.

BOOK FAIRS

Black Writers on Tour
Held annually. Check website for location and dates.

◉ **Leimert Park Village Book Fair**
0.5 Held in August.

BOOKS AND BOOKSTORES

◉ **LA Libreria**
3.0 *4732 W Washington Blvd, LA 90016.*

Malik Books:

◉ *3650 W. Martin Luther King Blvd. Suite #245. LA*
0.2 *90008.*

◉ *6000 Sepulveda Blvd, Suite 2470, Culver City*
4.8 *90230.*

◉ **Reparations Club**
2.8 *4636 W. Washington Blvd. LA. 90016.*

Shades of Africa
26.3
1001 E. 4th St., Long Beach. 90802.
Affordable Afrikan art, products, and books.

The Salt Eaters Bookshop
4.4
302 E. Queen St, Inglewood 90301.
Black owned. Woman-owned.

BOTANICAL GARDENS

See Arboretums and Gardens (i.e., Chinese, Japanese Gardens) for more botanic-related information.

Descanso Botanical Gardens
19.8
1418 Descanso Dr, La Cañada Flintridge 91011.

Japanese Botanical Garden
18.1
1151 Oxford Rd, San Marino 91108.
At the Huntington Library, Art museum and Botanical gardens.

LA Zoo Botanical Garden
13.6
5333 Zoo Dr, LA 90027

Manhattan Beach Botanical Garden
12.3
1237 N Peck Ave, Manhattan Beach 90266.
Located in Polliwog Park.

South Coast Botanic Garden
19.4
26300 Crenshaw Blvd, Palos Verdes Estates, 90274.
Koi pond.

UCLA Mildred E. Mathias Botanical Garden
10.8
707 Tiverton Dr, LA 90095.

BOWLING

Boliche means bowling in spanish. You'll find plenty of places to strike out near South LA.

Bowlero:

📍 *12125 Venice Blvd, LA 90066.*
6.4

📍 *8731 Lincoln Blvd, Westchester 90045.*
7.9

📍 **Gardena Bowling Center**
12.2 *15707 Vermont Ave, Gardena, 90247.*
Billiards and arcade also offers a pro shop, lounge & snack bar.

Lucky Strike:

📍 *800 W Olympic Blvd, LA 90015.*
6.3

📍 *6801 Hollywood Blvd, Hollywood, 90028.*
7.1

📍 **Shatto 39 Lanes**
5.8 *3255 W 4th St, LA 90020.*
Basic bowling alley featuring arcade games, several pool tables & a bar with beer, wine & cocktails.

📍 **The Spare Room**
7.2 7000 Hollywood Blvd, LA 90028.
Cocktail lounge & game parlor. Inside Hollywood Roosevelt Hotel.

📍 **XLanes LA**
7.3 *333 Alameda St, LA 90013.*

BREWERIES

Like beer? LA has dozens of breweries and craft beverage companies. Here's a few located near South LA. Search "breweries near me" to find more. See also Wine and Wineries.

Crowns & Hops
Black-owned. Search "crownsandhops" for more information.

South Los Angeles Beverage Company
Black-owned. Search "People's Republic of South Central" for more information.

📍 **Three Weavers Brewing Company**
5.3 *1031 W. Manchester Blvd A-B, Inglewood, CA 90301.*

Thunderhawk Alements
Black-owned. In San Diego. Search "thunderhawkbeer" for more information.

Warcloud Brewing
Black-owned. Search "warcloudbrewing" for more information.

C

CAFE'S AND COFFEE

Harun's Coffee + Cafe
0.8 *4336 Degnan Blvd, LA 90008.*

Highly Unlikely Cafe
4310 W Jefferson Blvd, LA 90016.
1.3 Dishes up delicious eats, coffee, beer and wine.

Hilltop Coffee, Cafe + Kitchen:

4427 W Slauson Ave, LA 90043.
2.4

170 N. La Brea Ave, Inglewood, 90301.
4.3

Hot and Cool Coffee + Cafe
0.7 *4331 Degnan Blvd, LA 90008*

LA Grind Coffee & Tea Bar
3.6 *1412 S Redondo Blvd, LA, 90019.*

Sip and Sonder
4.7 *108 S Market Street Inglewood, 90301.*

OG Cannabis Cafe

6.5   *1201 N La Brea, West Hollywood 90038.*
Serving farm fresh food, coffee, juice and cannabis daily. Sit on the patio, order a meal, have a conversation and experience cannabis.

South LA Cafe

1.3   *3991 S Western Ave, LA 90062.*

Tak's Coffee Shop

0.5   *3870 Crenshaw Blvd #101, LA 90008.*
Hawaiian and Asian influenced dishes.

Vee's Cafe

1.3   *5418 W Adams Blvd, LA 90016.*

CAJUN AND CREOLE CUISINE

See Restaurants for more food, dining and restaurant-related options.

Harold and Belle's New Orleans Restaurant & Lounge

1.5   2920 W Jefferson Blvd, LA 90018. New Orleans in LA.

La Louisianne Cajun Creole Soul Food Restaurant

2.6   *5812 Overhill Dr, LA 90043.*
Po' boys, catfish & jambalaya are some of the items at this Creole spot with nightly live jazz.

Orleans and York Deli + Cajun Cafe:

4.0 *400 E Florence Ave Inglewood 90301.*

0.4 *3868 Crenshaw Blvd LA 90008.*

2.7 *4454 W Slauson Ave, Windsor Hills 90043.*

Simply D'Licious
2.5 *4641 W Washington Blvd, LA 90016.*

The Little Jewel of New Orleans Grocery & Deli Restaurant
8.4 *207 Ord St, LA 90012.*
Southern-styled market and delicatessen draws its influence from the City of New Orleans.

CANDY

See's Candy Factory
2.6 *3431 S La Cienega Blvd, LA 90016.*

CANNABIS

There is more cannabis in South LA than you can shake a spliff at.

California Cannabis
2.7 *7415 Crenshaw Blvd, LA 90043.*
Black owned.

Gorilla Rx Wellness
4233 S Crenshaw Blvd, LA 90008.
0.3　Black owned cannabis.

LA Cannabis Company:

1.4　*3791 2nd Ave, LA, CA 90018*

3.4　*1603 S South La Brea Ave, LA, CA 90019*

3.4　*5993 S St Andrews Pl, LA, CA 90047*

OG Cannabis Cafe
1201 N La Brea, West Hollywood 90038.
6.5　America's first, and only, marijuana dispensary + and cafe.

The High Note
2.0　*5277 W Jefferson Blvd. LA 90016.*

CAPOEIRA

Want to learn Capoeira? There are several good Capoeira schools in and around South LA.

Capoeira Batuque
12453 Washington Blvd, LA 90066.
7.1　At Brasil Brasil Cultural Center.

Capoeira Besouro
9.6　*709 Lincoln Blvd, Venice 90291.*

📍 **Capoeira Brasil LA**
3.6 *5557 Washington Blvd, LA 90016.*

CARIBBEAN CUISINE

See Cuban Cuisine, Jamaican Food and Restaurants for more options.

📍 **Blessed Tropical Cuisine**
4.5 *4233 Crenshaw Blvd, LA 90008.*

📍 **Lee's Caribbean**
4.7 *4233 Crenshaw Blvd, LA 90008.*

📍 **Rosalie's Caribbean Cuisine**
4.6 *446 S Market St #2310, Inglewood 90301.* See also Shabazz Bakery.

CARIBBEAN MARKET

📍 **Right Choice Caribbean Market**
0.2 *4233 Crenshaw Blvd, LA 90008.*

📍 **Stone's Grocery and Market**
2.4 *6700 Crenshaw Blvd, LA 90043.*

CAROUSELS

📍 **Griffith Park Merry-Go-Round**
14.8 *4730 Crystal Springs Dr, LA 90027.*
Built in 1926, features 68 elaborately decorated horses & an organ.

Pelican Pier Pavillion Arcade and Carousel
25.1 *411 Shoreline Village Drive, Long Beach, 90802.*

Looff Hippodrome Carousel
1624 Ocean Front Walk, Santa Monica 90401.
10.7 On the Pier.

Tom Mankiewicz Conservation Carousel
16.7 *5333 Zoo Dr, LA 90027.*

CASINOS

Commerce Casino
6121 Telegraph Rd, Commerce 90040.
11.8 Crowne Plaza Hotel.

Crystal Casino
17.8 *123 E Artesia Blvd, Compton 90220.*

Hollywood Park Casino
3883 W Century Blvd, Inglewood, 90303.
5.5 Casino and sports bar.

Hustler Casino
11.8 *1000 W Redondo Beach Blvd, Gardena 90247.*

Larry Flynt's Lucky Lady Casino
11.1 *1045 Rosecrans Ave, Gardena 90247.*

The Bicycle Hotel & Casino
11.8 *888 Bicycle Casino Dr, Bell Gardens 90201.*

The Gardens Casino
25.6 *11871 E Carson St, Hawaiian Gardens 90716.*

CAVES

See Walking Paths and Trails, etc,... for more information about walking paths and trails.

Bronson Caves aka The Bat Cave
3200 Canyon Drive, LA 90068.
8.8   Featured in the 1970's TV version of Batman, this 0.6 mile heavily trafficked out and back trail features a cave and is good for all skill levels. Dog-friendly.

Cave of Munits
24501 Vanowen St, West Hills, 91307.
30.0   Hiking & rock-climbing locale with a series of caves & elevated sunset views.

Corral Canyon Cave
30.0   *Mesa Peak Motorway, Agoura Hills, CA 91301.*

Vanalden Cave
25.7   *Vanalden Cave Trail, Tarzana, 91356.*

CHICKEN

Cajun and Creole Cuisine, Fried Chicken, Restaurants, and Soul Food for more chicken related information.

Jerusalem Chicken
4448 W Slauson, LA 90043.
2.6   A Palestinian Chicken Eatery.

Harold's Chicken & Bar
6.6   *6523 Hollywood Blvd, LA 90028.*

CHINATOWN

See Cities and Neighborhoods Around South LA for more information.

📍 **Chinatown Central Plaza**
8.9   *943 N Broadway, LA 90012.*

CHINESE GARDEN

📍 **Garden of Flowing Fragrance**
1151 Oxford Rd, San Marino 91108.
18.1   At the Huntington Library, Art Museum and Botanical Gardens.

CIGAR LOUNGES

📍 **Cuban Leaf Cigar Lounge**
3.7   *424 E. Florence Ave. Inglewood, 90301.*

📍 **Drobe Stogies**
3.2   *1322 N. La Brea Ave, Inglewood, 90302.*

📍 **The Debonair Cigar Lounge**
3.9   *1111 S. La Brea Ave, LA 90019.*

CITIES AND NEIGHBORHOODS AROUND SOUTH LA

See Mexico for additional locations.

Beverly Hills
7.6
Home to celebrities, luxury hotels, a restaurant row and Rodeo Drive. The Beverly Hills Gardens Park features fountains and a rose garden. Population 33,709; 1.5% Black (2020).

Chinatown
8.8
Festive location. Lot's of places to eat and shop. See art galleries, the Taoist Temple, East Gate and the Golden Pagoda. Make a wish at the Seven Star Cavern Wishing Well. Population: 16,557; 1.5% Black (2020).

Compton
11.8
Known as the Hub City, Compton is home to Compton/Woodley Airport, Compton College, the Compton Golf Course, the Crystal Casino, the Dominguez Rancho Adobe Museum and Tomorrow's Aeronautical Museum. Compton has served as a creative base for Eazy-E, Ice-Cube, Dr. Dre, Snoop Dogg and Kendrick Lamar and many others. Population: 95,804; 27.1% Black (2020).

Crenshaw AKA the Crenshaw District
0.0
South LA's Crenshaw District is the cultural center of Black Los Angeles. Known to the hip-hop generation as the "Shaw", Crenshaw is a world-famous destination renowned for its multiculturalism, creativity, rebellious spirit, dynamism, hip-hop royalty and afrocentricity.

Culver City

4.0
Adjacent to the Baldwin Hills/Crenshaw community, Culver City is home to movie studios, screenland tours, a buzzing dining and nightlife scene, gastropubs and cozy cocktail bars. Population: 41,159; 8.7% Black (2020).

El Segundo

10.4
This small beachside city serves as the headquarters for many of LA's professional sports teams and is home to the aerospace industry, gastropubs, breweries and the beach.. Hometown on the TV show Sanford and Son. Population: 16,575; 4.7% Black. (2021).

Hermosa Beach

13.7
Hermosa Beach 90254. Population: 19,147; 0.5% Black (2021).

Hollywood

10.0
Home to the Hollywood Sign, the Hollywood Bowl, Universal Studios Hollywood and the Hollywood Walk of Fame. Tons of fun and things to do from $ to $$$$. Population: 62,953; 9.0% Black. (2021).

Inglewood

4.7
Forum, Hollywood Park Casino, SoFi Entertainment Complex, and cool places to eat. Inglewood's Market Street district has art galleries, book stores, the Inglewood Senior Center and the light rail Florence Boulevard station. Search for Inglewood City Public Art to learn more about the city's art installations. Population: 109,309; 40.1 Black (2021).

Korea Town

4.8

LA is home to one of the largest Korean communities outside of Korea. With numerous restaurants, grills, boba joints, karaoke spots, dance clubs, health spas, concert venues and a 24/7 vibe, you can find something new to do around the clock. Population: 120,000; 9.0% Black. (2021). See Korean Food and Korean Friendship Bell for more information.

Las Vegas, Nevada

273

Just 40 minutes away by airplane and 4 hours by car, Las Vegas is closer to South LA than San Francisco. With vibrant nightlife, great shows, a range of restaurants and lady luck, you are sure to have fun in Vegas. Population: 646,790; 11.5% Black (2021)

Leimert Park

0.6

Dubbed the "Black Greenwich Village" by filmmaker John Singleton, Leimert Park is the heart of LA's African American cultural community. Leimert Park showcases the best of Black LA. Check out the monthly Leimert Art Walk. Shop for art, fashion and jewelry. Have a cup of coffee. Try the BBQ, spicy Jamaican cuisine, vegan cuisine or tantalizing soul food. 43rd and Degnan. Population: 44,272; 55.14% Black (2021).

Little Tokyo Historic District

7.4

Heart of the largest Japanese-American population in North America. Population: 39,709; 13.26% Black. (2021).

Long Beach

20.0

Cool waterfront. Walkable art-filled downtown. Population: 456,062; 12.1% Black (2021).

Los Angeles (LA)

Founded on September 4, 1781. LA's official name is Nuestra Señora La Reina de los Angeles de Porciuncula, which translates to 'Our Lady the Queen of the Angels of Porciuncula' in English. Twenty-six of the 44 original settlers (pobladores) were African/Black, African/Black + Indian or African/Black + Other). Most came from Sinaloa, Mexico, where two-thirds of the residents were people of mixed African and Spanish heritage. Although eclipsed by new immigrants in the early American years, by 1930 LA was home to the largest Pan-African/Black community on the Pacific Coast. Population: 3,849, 297; 8.6% Black (2021).

Manhattan Beach

11.5 Home to Bruce's Beach, the site of one of the only Black owned beach resorts in the 1920's. The ownership rights were returned to the family in 2022. Check out the bike path, the Strand, the aquarium and one of the best piers in Southern California. Population: 35,064 (2020). Population: 35,064; 0.5% Black (2020).

Marina Del Rey

10.0 Population: 20,065; 4.9% Black (2020).

Mount Baldy

53.0 Population: 441; 5.8% Black (2021).

Oceanside

90.2 Great weather. Gorgeous beaches. Wooden pier. New England-style harbor. Check out the Oceanside Sunset Market every Thursday, it's one of the very best in Southern California. Population: 175,694; 4.7% Black (2021).

Playa Del Rey

12.0 Population: 16,230; 3.9% Black (2020).

Redondo Beach

14.0 Fifteen parks, recreational harbor, pier and Seaside Lagoon. Population: 69,871; 3.1% Black (2021).

San Diego

126 Known for its beaches, parks, and warm climate. Population: 1,381,611; 6.0% Black (2021).

Santa Monica

10.2 Coastal city overlooking the Pacific Ocean. Population: 91,105; 4.5% Black (2021).

Skid Row

8.0 A DTLA neighborhood. Population: est. 6000; 58.21% Black (2019).

Thai Town

13.6 Only designated "Thai Town" in the U.S. Try Thai Food and Thai Yoga. At Hollywood Blvd and N Kingley Dr. Population: 5,328; 3.1% Black (2019).

View Park-Windsor Hills

1.5 Has the highest concentration of African Americans in California. Population: 11,621; 77.52% Black (2020).

Venice

9.3 Funky little beach community where gentrification has gone wild. Check out the boardwalk, pier and canal district. Venice 90292. Pop.: 37,705; 5.4% Black (2000).

Watts

12.7 Historic South Central LA community. 90002. Population: 36,815; 37.1% Black (2000).

Westwood Village

9.8 Walkable historic district with movie theater, restaurants and shops. Home of UCLA. Population: 47,916; 2.0% Black (2000).

Willowbrook

11.3 Home to MLK Jr. Medical Center, Augustus Hawkins Mental Health Center, Charles Drew University, King/Drew High School, LA Metro Train Station and the Willowbrook Library. Population: 24,401; 34.4% Black (2010).

CITY HALL

LA City Hall
7.0 *200 N Spring St, LA 90012.*

CLIMBING

Cliffs of Id
3.2 *2537 S Fairfax Ave, Culver City 90232.* Climbing walls.

COLLEGES

Refer to Universities to find more information on South LA's institutions of higher learning.

Compton College
18.0 *1111 E Artesia Blvd, Compton 90221.*

Los Angeles City College
7.2 *855 N Vermont Ave, LA 90029.*

📍 **Los Angeles Southwest College**
7.2 *1600 W Imperial Hwy, LA 90047.*

📍 **Los Angeles Trade–Technical College**
6.1 *400 W Washington Blvd, LA 90015.*

📍 **Otis College of Art and Design**
7.2 *9045 Lincoln Blvd, LA 90045.*

📍 **West LA College**
4.9 *9000 Overland Ave, Culver City 90230.*

COMEDY

📍 **Sugar Shack**
1843 W Imperial Hwy, LA, CA 90047.
5.2 Casual outdoor comedy venue.

📍 **The Lexington Bar**
129 E 3rd St, LA 90013.
5.7 Live music and comedy venue with a creative vibe in the heart of downtown LA.

COMPTON

See Cities and Neighborhoods Around South LA for more information.

CONCERT VENUES

See Entertainment Centers, Festivals, Performing Arts and Theaters for more concert-related information.

📍 **Hollywood Bowl**
8.3 *2301 N Highland Ave, LA 90068.*

📍 **Staples Center**
6.1 *1111 S Figueroa St, LA 90015.*

📍 **The Forum**
7.1 *3900 W Manchester Blvd, Inglewood 90305.*

CONCERT SERIES

In summertime, South LA is the place to be. Check out these mostly free Summer Concert Series. Parking usually isn't free.

📍 **Baldwin Hills Crenshaw Plaza Free Summer Concert Series**
0.3 *3650 W Martin Luther King Jr Blvd, LA, 90008.*

📍 **Burton Chace Park Summer Concert Series.**
8.4 *13650 Mindanao Way, Marina Del Rey.*

📍 **Grand Performances Summer Concert Series**
7.3 *350 S Grand Ave. , LA, 90071.*

📍 **Levitt Pavilion - 50 Free Summer Concerts**
2230 W 6th St, LA, CA 90057.
6.4 Outdoor performance space in McArthur Park, hosting free summer concerts by emerging & name artists.

📍 **LA County Museum of Art - Jazz at LACMA Series**
5.5 *5905 Wilshire Blvd, LA, 90036.*

LA County Museum of Art - LACMA Latin Sounds Music Series

5.5

5905 Wilshire Blvd, LA 90036.
Generally runs late May through the end of August.

Santa Monica Pier Summer Concert Series - Twilight on the Pier

11.6

Free weekly music festival every Wed, Aug 21-Sept 25, now in it's 35th consecutive year, featuring art, an all new comedy stage, eats, wine and beer garden, games and interactive activations.

COOKIES

See Bakeries and Ice Cream for more cookie-related information.

CREATIVE SPACES

KAOS Network

0.9

4343 Leimert Blvd., LA 90008.
One of the most dynamic spaces in South LA.

The Metaphor Club

0.6

4333 Crenshaw Blvd, LA 90008.
A creative lounge where writers, creators, and intellectuals could gather to work.

CRENSHAW

See Cities and Neighborhoods Around South LA for more information.

CUBAN CUISINE

See Restaurants for more food, dining and restaurant-related options.

📍 **Floridita Restaurant**
6.2 *1253 Vine St, LA 90038.*
Serves authentic Cuban and caribbean inspired cuisine daily for lunch and dinner.

Versailles Cuban Restaurant
Offering traditional Cuban dishes

📍 *10319 Venice Blvd, LA 90034.*
4.5

📍 *1415 S La Cienega Blvd, LA 90035.*
4.7

CULTURAL CENTERS

See Art Centers and Performing Arts for more culture-related information.

📍 **African American Cultural Center**
0.4 *3018 W 48th St, LA 90043.*
Promotes knowledge and appreciation of African American culture.

Black Cultural Events Website
Afrocentric events.

Brasil Brasil Cultural Center
12453 Washington Blvd, LA 90066.
7.1
Offers classes in Capoeira, Samba, Zumba Hip-Hop, Drumming and Dance.

City of Los Angeles Department of Cultural Affairs
201 N Figueroa St #1400, LA 90012.
Refer to the website for more information.

Japanese American Cultural Center
244 San Pedro St, LA 90012.
8.4
A hub for Japanese and Japanese American arts and culture and a community gathering place for the diverse voices it inspires.

Korean Cultural Center
5505 Wilshire Blvd, LA, 90036.
4.1
Experience the rich traditions and history of Korea through specialized programs, sponsored events, and multiple learning resources.

The Little Ethiopia Cultural and Resource Center
1037 S Fairfax Ave, LA, 90019.
4.9
Works to advance the social, economic and cultural well-being of Ethiopians and other communities in LA.

Los Angeles Chinese Cultural Center
1110 Bates Ave, LA, 90029.
6.8
The Los Angeles Chinese Cultural Center (LACCC) was founded in 2005 in the Hollywood area to enrich the community by providing various Chinese cultural programs for all ages.

○ **Skirball Cultural Center**
11.9 *2701 N Sepulveda Blvd, LA, 90049.*

○ **Torrance Cultural Arts Center**
13.9 *3330 Civic Center Dr, Torrance, CA 90503.*

○ **Vision Theater - Designated Cultural Arts Center**
0.8 *3341 W 43rd Place, LA 90008.*

○ **Watts Towers Arts Center - Designated Cultural Center**
10.5 *3330 Civic Center Dr, Torrance, CA 90503.*

○ **William Grant Still Arts Center - Designated Cultural Arts Center**
2.1 *4321 Degnan Blvd, LA 90008.*
An educational and performance art space in

CULVER CITY

See Cities and Neighborhoods Around South LA for more information.

D

DANCE

📍 **Crenshaw Dance and Yoga**
1.7 *5426 Crenshaw Blvd, LA 90043.*

📍 **Debbie Allen Dance Academy**
3.4 *1850 S Manhattan Pl, LA 90019*

📍 **Lula Washington Dance Theater**
0.5 *3773 Crenshaw Blvd, LA 90016.*

📍 **Viver Brasil Dance Company**
7.5 *2141 N Gower St., LA 90068.*

DISC GOLF

Like frisbee? Like golf?

📍 **Chavez Ridge Disc Golf Course**
10.0 *Solano Canyon Dr & Park Row Drive, LA 90012.*

📍 **De Bell Disc Golf Course**
13.5 *1500 E. Walnut Ave., Burbank, 91501.*

📍 **Kenneth Hahn State Park Disc Golf Course**
2.4 *4100 S La Cienega Blvd, LA 90056.*

DOG PARKS

Boneyard Dog Park
3.6 *Duquesne Ave, Culver City 90230.*

Glen Alla Dog Park
7.0 *4601 Alla Rd. Marina Del Rey 90292.*

Westminster Dog Park
9.9 *1234 Pacific Avenue Venice 90291.*

DONUTS

There are dozens of doughnut shops in South LA but only one has a giant donut on top of it.

Randy's Donuts
805 West Manchester Blvd, Inglewood, CA 90301.
5.4 Three 3 locations in South LA, only the original location features the iconic giant donut. Get a t-shirt and take a picture.

Krispy Kreme Donuts
4034 Crenshaw Blvd, LA 90008.
0.1 See 'em made through the glass window. Kids 12 and under get one free donut per visit.

DRUMS/DRUMMING

Regular drum circles are held in Leimert Park and other locales. If you don't know where—ask somebody with a drum.

African Marketplace & Drum Circle
43rd and Degnan, LA 90008.
3.6 Sundays 10 am to 5 pm.

Motherland Music Drums
601 N Eucalyptus Ave, Inglewood 90302.
4.1 African drums and supplies, custom drum making, repairs and maintenance, instruction and performances.

Rhythm Arts Alliance
4343 Leimert Blvd. LA 90008.
0.7 Community Drum classes most Monday nights at the KAOS Network.

E

EARTHQUAKE FAULT ZONE

 Newport-Inglewood Fault Zone (NIFZ)
3.9   This 47 mile long fault starts in Culver City and runs
through Inglewood and Newport Beachtowards the
Pacific Ocean.

EGYPTIAN FOOD

See Restaurants for more food, dining and restaurant-related
options.

Tut's Egyptian Cuisine
7.2   *12114 W Washington Blvd, LA 90066.*

EL SEGUNDO

See Cities and Neighborhoods Around South LA for more
information.

ENTERTAINMENT CENTERS

LA LIVE
6.2
800 Olympic Blvd, LA 90015.
Huge entertainment complex with music, sports, dining and more. Adjacent to the Staples Center and the Convention Center.

Savoy Entertainment Center
4.5
218 South La Brea Ave, Inglewood, 90301.
Located in DT Inglewood, the premier choice for LA's urban trendsetters.

Sofi Stadium and Entertainment Complex
4.8
1001 Stadium Dr, Inglewood 90301.

EQUESTRIAN CENTERS

Like horse riding?

Bay Ridge Equestrian
15.9
7221 Cortland Ave, Paramount 90723.
Horse riding school in Paramount, California.

Griffith Park Horse Rentals
17.5
1820 Riverside Dr, Glendale 91201.
Equestrian center offering guided park & mountain trail rides for various ages & levels.

LA Equestrian Center
13.8
480 Riverside Dr, Burbank 91506.
Horseback riding lessons, trail rides & boarding in a pastoral setting.

ESSENTIAL OILS

Lot's of places to get oils in South LA but nobody's been around as long as ZamZam.

ZamZam Perfumes and Essential Oils
4293 Crenshaw Blvd, LA 90008.
0.4   Essential oils, incense, soaps, African/Asian products.

ETHIOPIAN FOOD

See Industry Cafe & Jazz, pg. 95; Queen of Sheba Ethiopian Restaurant pg. 145; and Little Ethiopia.

EXERCISE

See Beaches, Bike Paths, Health, Hiking, Parks, Walking Paths, Trails, for more information.

Crenshaw Family YMCA
3820 Santa Rosalia Dr, LA 90008.
0.4   Facilities include Basketball Courts, Weight Room. Programs feature a variety of activities for youth, adults and seniors.

Thrive Health Lab (THL)
3701 W. 54th St, LA 90043.
1.6   Fitness, nutrition and mental, physical, and financial wellbeing.

F

FARMERS MARKETS

African Marketplace Farmers Market
43rd and Degnan, LA 90008.
0.5   Sundays 10 am to 5 pm.

Crenshaw Farmers Market
Located on the grounds of the BHCP mall.
0.2   Saturday 10 am to 3 pm.

Inglewood Farmers Market
4.5   *Market St and Manchester Blvd, Inglewood 90301.*

Ladera Farmers Market
3.8   *5453 W Slauson Ave, LA 90056.*

Los Angeles Farmers Market
5.8   *6333 W 3rd St, LA 90036.*

Wellington Square Farmers Market
2.5   *4394 W Washington Blvd, LA 90016.*

FESTIVALS

Central Avenue Jazz Festival
4222 S Central Ave, LA 90011.
4.9   Held annually in July.

Day of the Drum Festival
1727 E. 107th St. LA 90002.
12.8　At Watts Towers. Annually in September.

Juneteenth
43rd and Degnan.
0.8　Annually in June.

Leimert Park Jazz Festival
4020 Marlton Ave, LA 90008.
0.2　Annually in August.

Pan African Film Festival (PAFF)
4020 Marlton Ave, LA 90008.
0.2　Annually in February.

Samba in the Streets
4343 Leimert Blvd, LA, CA 90008.
0.8　Visit the "Viver Brasil" website for information.

Simon Rodia Jazz Festival
1727 E. 107th St. LA 90002.
12.8　At Watts Towers. Annually in September.

Pan African Film Festival (PAFF)
4020 Marlton Ave, LA 90008.
0.0　Annually in February.

FISHING

See Sportfishing for more fish-related information.

Earvin Magic Johnson Park Lake
10.9　*1050 E 120th St, LA 90059.*

Kenneth Hahn State Recreation Area Lake

2.3   *4100 S. La Cienega Blvd, LA 90056.*

FLOWERS

So many flower shops, so little time. The most amazing are in DTLA.

 Lopez Flowers

1.7   *3409 S. La Brea Blvd. LA 90016.*

 Los Angeles Flower Mart

6.8   *754 Wall St, LA 90014.*

FOOD

See Restaurants for more food, dining and restaurant-related options.

FORESTS

 Angeles National Forest, Los Angeles River Ranger District Office

32.3   *12371 Little Tujunga Canyon Rd, Sylmar 91342.*
Mountainous national forest covering 700,000-acres with chaparral, pine & fir trees & hiking trails.

 Old Santa Monica Forestry Station

13.4   *178 Latimer Rd, Santa Monica 90402.*
First experimental forestry station in the US. California Historic Landmark #840.

FRENCH BAKERY

See Bakeries and Restaurants for more information.

FRENCH DIP SANDWICHES

See Restaurants for more food, dining and restaurant-related options.

📍 **Cole's French Dip Restaurant and Bar**
7.1 *118 E. 6th St, LA 90014.*

📍 **Philippe's "The Original" Restaurant**
8.5 *1001 N. Alameda, LA 90012.*

FRIES

Mr. Fries Man
World-famous. Black-owned.

📍 *3844 S Figueroa St, LA 90037.*
3.8

📍 *1120 W Florence Ave #C, Inglewood 90301.*
5.3

📍 *14800 S Western Ave #108, Gardena 90249.*
9.4

FRIED CHICKEN

See Cajun and Creole, Restaurants and Soul Food for more dining and restaurant-related options.

Dave's Hot Chicken
3.5 *5301 W Centinela Ave, LA 90045.*
East Hollywood-borne chain.

Gus's World Famous Fried Chicken
2.8 *1262 Crenshaw Blvd, LA 90019.*
Memphis-borne chain.

Harold's Chicken & Bar
6.6 *6523 Hollywood Blvd, LA 90028.*

Roscoe's House of Chicken and Waffles
World-famous. Black-owned.

5.1 *621 W. Manchester Blvd, Inglewood 90301.*

6.7 *1514 N. Gower St, Hollywood.*

3.5 *5006 Pico Blvd, LA 90019.*

Sweet Chick's Fried Chicken
6.4 *448 N. Fairfax Ave, LA 90036.*

G

GARDENS

See Arboretums, Art Parks, Botanical Gardens, Chinese Garden, Japanese Gardens, Rose Garden and Sculpture Gardens, Nature Centers, Museums, Parks, Preserves, Wetlands and Wildlife Refuges, etc for more garden-related information.

Getty Center Central Garden
13.6   *1200 Getty Center Dr, LA 90049.*

Koreatown Pavilion & Garden
1000 Normandie Ave, LA, 90006.
4.7   Dawooljong is the 5,000-square-foot pavilion and garden at Olympic Boulevard and Normandie Avenue. It is across the street from where Koreatown began in the late 1960s with a Korean grocery store. Made of pine and dyed in traditional shades of green, rust and red, the open-air pavilion is topped by an upswept tiled roof. Called Da Wool Jung , meaning a harmonious gathering place, the monument was built by South Korean craftsmen who were brought here for the job.

LA River Center & Gardens
570 W Ave 26 #100, LA 90065.
10.1   A hidden jewel, sequestered behind thick, ivy covered walls. A wide, circular brick driveway with a spreading ficus tree in the center marks the entrance, and through the arched, wrought-iron gate you get your first glimpse of the fountains, flowers and serenity inside.

📍 **Peace Awareness Labyrinth and Gardens**
2.0   *3500 W Adams Blvd, LA 90018.*
Headquarters of the Movement of Spiritual Inner
Awareness, dedicated to exploring peace and practical
spirituality. Free

📍 **Rancho Los Alamitos Historic Ranch and Gardens**
27.3   See "Adobes" for more information.

📍 **West Athens Victory Garden**
6.7   *1344 W 105th St, LA, 90044.*

GARDEN TOURS

Leimert Park Garden Tour
Biennial self-guided tour.

GOLF

With so many public links close to South LA, you'll have no
problems keeping up your golf game.

📍 **Alondra Golf Course**
9.0   *16400 Prairie Ave. Lawndale, 90260.*
This course has two 18 hole courses including a par 3,
18 hole short course.

📍 **Chester Washington Golf Course**
7.6   *1818 Charlie Sifford Dr, LA 90047.*

📍 **Lakes at El Segundo Golf Course**
9.3   *400 S Sepulveda Blvd, El Segundo 90245.*
Municipal 9-hole golf course offering a driving range,
lessons & a cafe.

Maggie Hathaway Golf Course
1921 W 98th St, LA 90047.
6.0 A 9 hole par 3 course located within Jesse Owens Park.

Penmar Golf Course
9.6 *1233 Rose Ave, Venice, 90291.*

Rancho Park Golf Course
7.5 *10460 W Pico Blvd, LA, 90064.*

Victoria Golf Course
340 MLK Jr. St. Carson, 90746.
11.0 An LA County Parks and Recreation facility.

Westchester Golf Course
7.1 *6900 W Manchester Ave, LA 90045.*

GREEK FOOD

Mizlala West Adams
5400 West Adams Blvd, LA 90016.
2.6 Local neighborhood mediterranean grill.

Papa Christo's Greek Restaurant, Deli and Taverna
2771 Pico Blvd, LA 90006.
4.5 Market & no-frills restaurant

GROUND ZERO

Ground Zero
The intersection of Florence and Normandie in South
4.9 LA is considered to be "ground zero" of the 1992 South
LA Rebellion.

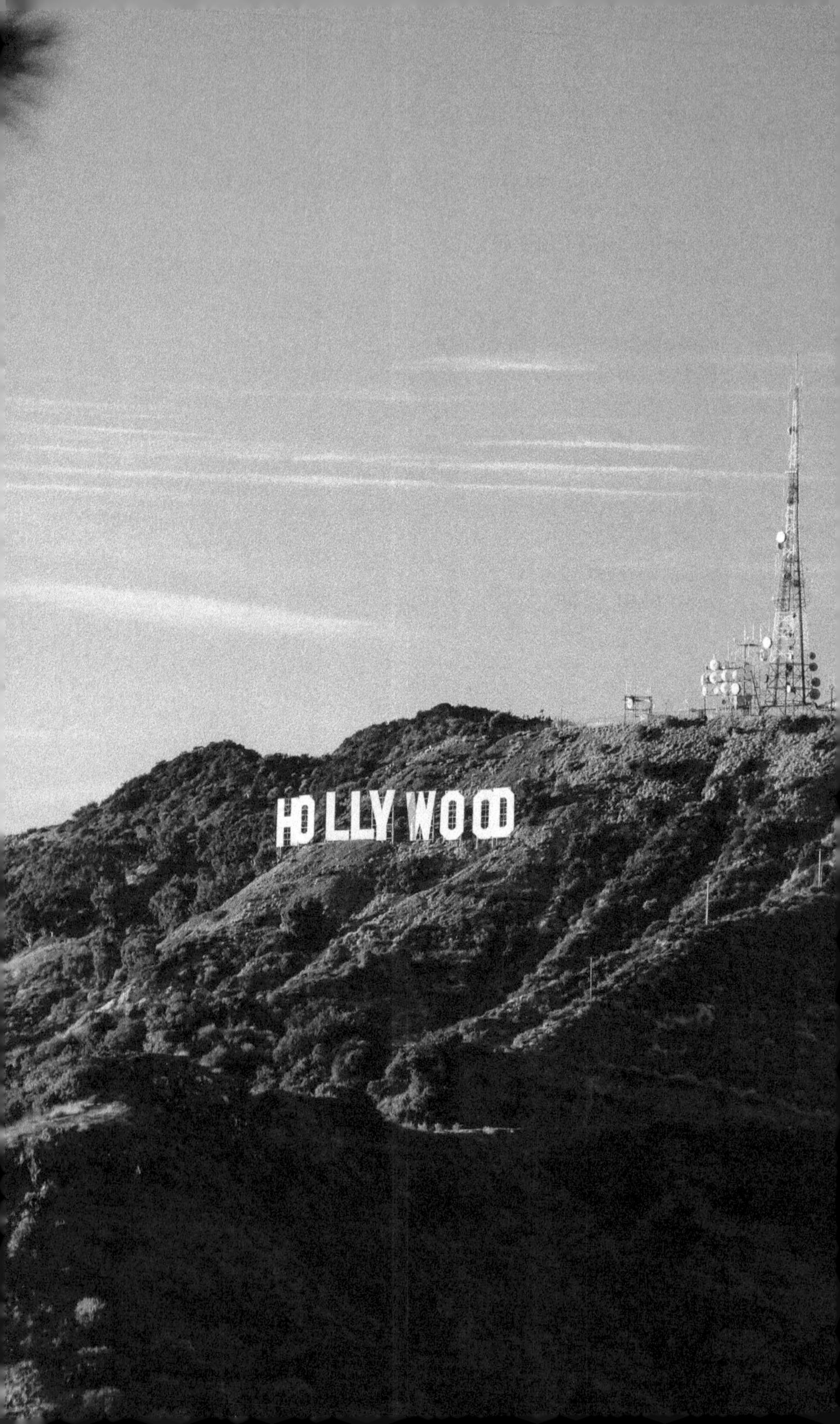

H

HALAL CUISINE

See Restaurants for more food, dining and restaurant-related options.

Banadir Somali Restaurant
5.2 *137 Arbor Vitae St, Inglewood 90301.*

Halal Food
1905 S Western Ave, LA 90018.
3.3 Indian.

Halal Kabob House
1117 W Manchester Blvd, Unit G, Inglewood 90301.
5.5 Pakistani.

Hummus House
12211 Hawthorne Blvd, Hawthorne 90250.
6.8 Mediterranean.

India's Tandoori Halal Restaurant
12866 Hawthorne Blvd, Hawthorne 90250.
7.8 Indian and Pakistani.

Mutiara Food & Market
225 S La Brea Ave, Inglewood 90301.
3.3 Indonesian and Malaysian.

Quebobs Mediterranean Restaurant
3560 S La Cienega Blvd, Unit F, LA 90016.
2.5

📍 **Ray's Halal Texas BBQ**
7.7   *6038 Santa Fe Ave, Huntington Park 90225.*

📍 **Soriana Halal Restaurant**
      512 E Washington Blvd, LA 90015.
5.4   Arabian.

HANGLIDING

📍 **Windsports Hang Gliding**
      12601 Vista Del Mar, Venice, 90293.
11.8 Lessons, advanced soaring, and pilot training at
      Dockweiler Beach.

HARBOR CRUISES

So many cruise companies, Google Harbor Cruises to find one that
suits your needs.

📍 **Catalina Express**
      Address Here
28.8 A nice way to get to Catalina Island.

📍 **King Harbor Marina**
14.4 *208 Yacht Way, Redondo Beach 90277.*

📍 **LA World Cruise Center**
      100 Swinford St. Wilmington 90744.
22.8 West Coast's largest cruise port.

📍 **Marina Del Rey Harbor**
      13755 Fiji Way, MDR 90292.
8.6   North America's largest man-made small-craft harbor.

HEALTH FOOD

Simply Wholesome Health Food Restaurant + Store
4508 W Slauson Ave, LA 90043.
2.6   Tasty, nutritious food and health products.

HEALTH AND HEALTHCARE

Dharma Health Institute
143 Culver Blvd, Playa Del Rey 90293.
9.6   Acupuncture, Qi Gong, Tai Chi, and Yoga.

Nappily Naturals Beauty Apothecary
0.7   *4342 Degnan Blvd, LA 90008.*

HERMOSA BEACH

See Cities and Neighborhoods Around South LA for more information.

HIKING TRAILS

See Beaches, Bike Paths, Caves, Nature Parks and Preserves, Walking Paths, and Wetlands, for more about walking paths and hiking trails.

Angeles National Forest, LA River District Office
32.3   *12371 Little Tujunga Canyon Rd, Sylmar 91342.*

Baldwin Hills Scenic Overlook
6300 Hetzler Rd, Culver City 90232.
3.0   Hilltop park with views of DTLA.

Briar Summit Open Space Preserve

10.4 *LA 90046.*

Culver City Stairs

3.0 *6105 Hetzler Rd, Culver City, CA 90232*

Ferndell Nature Trail

13.7 *5375 Red Oak Dr, LA 90068.*

Forrestal Nature Preserve

27.9 *32201 Forrestal Dr, Rancho Palos Verdes 90275.*

Kenneth Hahn State Recreation Area

3.2 *4100 S. La Cienega Blvd, LA 90056*

Mt. Baldy Wilderness Preserve

52.1 *Barrett Stoddard Truck Trail, Claremont 91711.*

Park to Playa Trailhead

3.1 Thirteen mile trail from Baldwin Hills to the beach.

The Bat Cave Trail

8.8 *3200 Canyon Dr, LA 90068.*

Sepulveda Basin Wildlife Reserve

18.3 *6416 Woodley Ave, Van Nuys 91406.*

Stocker Corridor Trail

0.7 *Stocker St & Presidio Dr, LA 90008.*

Verdugo Mountains Open Space Preserve

23.0 *Oakmount View Dr, Glendale 91209.*

HISTORICALLY BLACK BEACHES

Dockweiler, Hermosa, Redondo, Venice and Santa Monica are probably the most popular beaches for African Americans. You'll be certain to see African Americans at any beach in LA County. Don't forget your sunscreen. See Beaches for more information.

Bruce's Beach
2600 Highland Ave, Manhattan Beach 90266.
11.9 Historic site of African American beach resort.

The Inkwell
Santa Monica 90401.
12.0 Site of historic African American beach formerly located near Tower 20 on Santa Monica Beach (at the end of Bay Street). Area is currently called Crescent Bay Park.

Venice Beach
1800 Ocean Front Walk, Venice 90291.
10.0 Already gentrified, Venice Beach used to be the home of a thriving black community but not so much anymore. Despite this, it remains one of the most popular places to visit.

HISTORICALLY BLACK COLLEGE/UNIVERSITY IN SOUTH LA

Charles Drew University of Medicine and Science
1731 E 120th St, LA 90059.
12.1 California's only historically black university.

HOLLYWOOD

See Cities and Neighborhoods Around South LA for more information.

HORSES

See Equestrian Centers for more information.

HORSE RACING

See Equestrian Centers for more information.

Santa Anita Park
285 W Huntington Dr, Arcadia 91007.
24.0 Live thoroughbred horse racetrack with bars and restaurants.

HOSPITALS

There are many hospitals in South LA including Centinela Hospital in Inglewood, Dignity Health near downtown LA, and Kaisers all over the place. If you have an emergency or need a hospital right away, call 911.

Martin Luther King Jr. Hospital
12.0 *1680 E 120th St, LA 90059.*

HOT DOGS

Earle's Grill Restaurant
0.5 *3864 Crenshaw Blvd, LA 90008.*

Pink's Hot Dogs - Famous Take-Out Hot Dog Stand (Hollywood)
6.0 *709 N La Brea Ave, LA 90038.*
Creatively topped dogs (some named for celebrities) draw long lines at this historic roadside spot.

HUMMUS

See Restaurants for more food, dining and restaurant-related options.

Hummus House
709 N La Brea Ave, LA 90038.
6.8 Mediterranean.

Hummus Republic
709 N La Brea Ave, LA 90038.
9.0 Mediterranean.

The Hummus Factory
6.3 *6081 Center Dr, Unit 218, LA 90045.*

ICE CREAM

Screamin' for ice cream? How about a paleta, raspado, shaved ice or fruit bar?

Ginger's Divine Ice Cream and Pops
Two locations.

6.3 *8430 W 3rd St, LA 90048*

7.2 *12550 W Washington Blvd, LA 90066.*

Happy Ice
7.0 *7324 Melrose Ave, LA 90046.*

Jamz Creamery
4.7 *231 E. Manchester Blvd, Inglewood 90301.*

Jayis Ice Cream, Raspados and Popsicles
4.7 *1100 W Florence Ave, LA 90044.*

La Michoacana Ricas Nieves y Paletas
4.6 *303 W Manchester Blvd, Inglewood 90301.*

Mateo's Ice Cream & Fruit Bars
4234 W Pico Blvd, LA 90019.
2.4 Paletas y nieve de frutas naturales.

New Orleans Snoballs
4452 W Slauson Ave, Windsor Hills 90043.
2.4   Shaved ice.

Sweet Lilly's
0.8   *4501 W MLK Jr Blvd, LA 90016.*

YogurtTalk
3650 W MLK Jr Blvd, LA 90008.
0.1   Fro-yo and ice cream.

INGLEWOOD

See Cities and Neighborhoods Around South LA for more information.

ISLANDS

LA County's two islands, Santa Catalina and San Clemente, are part of the eight-island group called the Channel Islands.

Avalon/Catalina Island
About 22 miles off-shore. Use the Catalina Express to
55.0   visit.

San Clemente Island
Off-limits to visitors, this isle was used for bombing
00.0   and missile testing by the U.S. Navy.

J

JAMAICAN FOOD

See Cuban Food, Caribbean Cuisine and Restaurants for more options.

Ackee Bamboo Jamaican Restaurant
0.5 *4305 Degnan Blvd, LA 90008.*

Country Style Jamaican Cuisine
3.6 *4305 Degnan Blvd, LA 90008.*

Island Reggae Kitchen
7.8 *14426 Crenshaw Blvd, Gardena 90249.*

Karuba's Yardy Kitchen
3.6 *4305 Degnan Blvd, LA 90008.*

Natraliart Jamaican Restaurant
2.7 *3426 W Washington Blvd, LA 90018.*
Caribbean standards served in hefty portions at this modest cafe with a colorful island mural.

JAPANESE FOOD

See Little Tokyo and Restaurants for more food, dining and restaurant-related options.

Yamashiro's Restaurant Hollywood (Japanese + Chinese)
7.7
1999 N Sycamore Ave, LA 90068.
Great restaurant, amazing food, beautifully appointed ground with a fantastic view of LA.

JAPANESE GARDENS

See Gardens, Arboretums and Sculpture Gardens for more information.

Earl Burns Miller Japanese Garden
Earl Warren Dr, Long Beach 90840.
27.0
On Cal State Long Beach campus.

Doris Japanese Garden
La Cienega Blvd, LA 90008.
4.1
In Kenneth Hahn Park.

Japanese Botanical Garden
1151 Oxford Rd, San Marino 91108.
18.1
At the Huntington Library, Art museum and Botanical gardens.

Japanese Garden
244 San Pedro St, LA 90012.
8.4
Inside the Japanese American Cultural Center.

Storrier Stearns Japanese Garden
15.2 *270 Arlington Dr, Pasadena, CA 91105.*

JAZZ

See Cultural Centers, Festivals and Radio for more information.

Barbara Morrison Performing Arts Center
0.4   *4305 Degnan Blvd, LA 90008.*

California Jazz and Blues Museum
0.7   *4317 Degnan Blvd, LA 90008.*

Central Avenue Jazz Festival
      4222 S Central Ave, LA 90011.
4.9   Annual July event held along Central Avenue between
      MLK Boulevard and Vernon Avenue.

Industry Cafe & Jazz
      6039 Washington Blvd, Culver City 90232.
3.4   Restaurant and jazz lounge. Ethiopian Food. Wine.
      Drinks.

Jazz/Latin Jazz at LACMA Series
See C for 'Concert Series' for more information.

Jazz on the Latin Side - KJAZZ 88.1
Friday's 8 pm to 11 pm. Saturday's 6 pm to 10 pm.

Leimert Park Jazz Festival
      4020 Marlton Ave, LA 90008.
3.4   Annually in August.

Pips on La Brea
      1356 S. La Brea Ave, LA 90019.
3.4   Restaurant. Bar. Wine. Live Jazz. Italian food.

Post and Beam - Restaurant and Bar

0.3 *3767 Santa Rosalia Dr, LA 90008.*
Restaurant. Bar. Patio. Frequent live jazz.

Simon Rodia Jazz Festival

12.8 Free performances throughout the day. Usually held on the last Sunday of September.

World Stage
See "Cultural Centers" for more information.

JEWELRY

Sika

0.6 *4330 Degnan Blvd, LA 90008.*
African style jewelry.

K

KAYAKING

See Rivers for additional information on LA's running waters.

LA River Expeditions (LARE)
LARE is the only outfitter to offer urban kayaking tours in both LA River recreational zones.   Book a tour online.

LA River Kayaks (LARK)
12.0 *2960 Marsh St, LA 90039.*

LA River Kayak Safari (LARKS)
11.6 *2825 Benedict St, LA 90039.*

UCLA Marina Aquatic Center (MAC)
9.1 *14001 Fiji Way, MDR 90292.*

KOREAN FOOD

Kang Nam - Traditional Korean Restaurant
4103 W Olympic Blvd, LA, 90019.
3.4
Traditional Korean & Japanese cuisine, from stews to sushi, served in a polished space with a patio.

KOREAN FRIENDSHIP BELL

📍
24.5

Korean Friendship Bell
3601 S Gaffey St, San Pedro, CA 90731.
Set under an ornate pagoda, this historic bell was a gift from Korea & has expansive sea views.

KOREA TOWN

See Cities and Neighborhoods Around South LA for more information.

L

LAKES

See Arboretums, Art Walks, Beaches, Bike Paths, Caves, Exercise, and Hiking Trails, Lakes, Nature Parks and Preserves, Walking Paths,Wetlands,etc,... for more info about walking paths and hiking trails.

Alondra Park Lake
12.4 *3850 Manhattan Beach Blvd, Lawndale 90260.*

Belvedere Park Lake
12.3 *4914 E 3rd St. East LA 90022.*

Big Bear Lake
105 *Big Bear Lake 92315.*

Castaic Lake
45.1 *Castaic 91384.*

Debs Lake
13.9 *4235 Monterey Rd, LA 90032.*

Earvin Magic Johnson Park Lake
10.9 *1050 E 120th St, LA 90059.*

Echo Park Lake
8.6 *751 Echo Park Ave, LA 90026.*

Lake Hollywood
LA 90068.

8.9   Views of Hollywood Sign.

Kenneth Hahn State Recreation Area Lake

2.3   *4100 S. La Cienega Blvd, LA 90056*

Lake Arrowhead

55.0   *Lake Arrowhead 92352.*

McArthur Park Lake

9.1   *653 S Alvarado St, LA 90057.*

Morningside Park Reservoir

1.0   *Inglewood 90305.*

Silverwood Lake Recreation Area

55.0   *14651 Cedar Circle, Hesperia 92345.*

LAS VEGAS, NEVADA

See Cities and Neighborhoods Around South LA for more information.

LEIMERT PARK

See Cities and Neighborhoods Around South LA for more information.

LIBRARIES

LA has the largest publicly funded library system in the U.S. Every branch has free Wi-Fi and computers that can be reserved for use.

African American Black Resource Center
10.7 *150 E. El Segundo Blvd, LA 90061.*

Black Hollywood Education and Resource Center
7.2 *1875 Century Park East, Suite 6th floor, LA 90067.*

Central Public Library DTLA
7.2 *630 W 5th St, LA, 90071.*

LA84 Foundation Sport History Library
2.9 *2141 W Adams Blvd, LA 90018.*

Ray Charles Memorial Library
3.6 *2107 W Washington Blvd, LA 90018.*

Southern California Library of South LA
4.5 *6120 S Vermont Ave, LA 90044.*
Holds extensive collections of histories of community resistance in LA and beyond.

Wanda Coleman Library
5.9 *120 W Florence Ave, LA 90003.*

A. C. Bilbrew Library
10.5 *150 E. El Segundo Blvd, LA 90061.*

Compton Library
14.1 *40 W Compton Blvd, Compton 90220.*

Julian Dixon Library
4.7 *4975 Overland Ave, Culver City 90230.*

Dr. Martin Luther King Jr Library

15.1   *17906 S Avalon Blvd, Carson, 90746.*

Lennox Library

6.4   *4359 Lennox Blvd, Lennox, 90304.*

Lloyd Taber-Marina del Rey Library

8.5   *4533 Admiralty Way, Marina del Rey 90292.*

View Park Bebe Moore Campbell Library

1.9   *3854 W 54th St, LA 90043.*

Willowbrook Library

11.3   *11737 Wilmington Ave, LA 90059.*

Woodcrest Library

7.3   *1340 W 106th St, LA, 90044.*

Angeles Mesa Library

1.6   *2700 W 52nd St, LA 90043.*

Baldwin Hills Branch Library

2.0   *2906 South La Brea Ave, LA 90016.*
A branch of the LA City Library system.

Mary McLeod Bethune Regional Library

1.9   *3900 S Western Ave, LA 90062.*

Frances Howard Goldwyn - Hollywood Regional Library

7.1   *1623 Ivar Ave, LA, CA 90028.*

Hyde Park Miriam Matthews Branch Library

3.9   *7150-7156 Arlington Ave, LA 90043.*

📍 **Jefferson Library**
2.1 *2211 W Jefferson Blvd, LA 90018.*

📍 **Mar Vista Branch Library**
10.0 *12006 CA-187, LA 90066.*

📍 **Abbot Kinney Memorial Branch Library**
9.6 *501 Venice Blvd, Venice, 90291.*

📍 **Vermont Square Branch Library**
3.4 *1201 W 48th St, LA 90037.*
The oldest branch library in the Los Angeles City Public Library system.

📍 **Washington Irving Branch Library**
2.3 *4117 W Washington Blvd, LA 90018.*

LITTLE TOKYO

See Cities and Neighborhoods Around South LA for more information.

LONG BEACH

See Cities and Neighborhoods Around South LA for more information.

LOS ANGELES

See Cities and Neighborhoods Around South LA for more information.

LOUNGES

Cuban Leaf Cigar Lounge
3.7 *424 E. Florence Ave. Inglewood, 90301.*

Harold and Belle's New Orleans Restaurant & Lounge
3.7 *2920 W. Jefferson Blvd, LA 90018.*

Industry Cafe & Jazz
3.4 *6039 Washington Blvd, Culver City 90232.*
Restaurant and jazz lounge. Ethiopian Food. Wine. Drinks.

Lavender Blue Restaurant & Lounge
3.9 *3310 W. Manchester Blvd, Inglewood, 90305.*
Jazz, blues and food.

The Debonair Cigar Lounge
3.9 *1111 S. La Brea Ave, LA 90019.*

The Wood Bar-B-Que and Sports Lounge
4.2 *129 N Market St, Inglewood 90301.*

The Spare Room
7.2 *7000 Hollywood Blvd, LA 90028.*
Cocktail lounge & game parlor. Inside Hollywood Roosevelt Hotel.

Metaphor Club
0.6 *4333 Crenshaw Blvd, LA 90008.*
Writer's lounge.

M

MANHATTAN BEACH

See Cities and Neighborhoods Around South LA for more information.

MARINA DEL REY

See Cities and Neighborhoods Around South LA for more information

MARKETS

See also Farmers Markets, Shopping and Shopping Malls for more information.

Grand Central Market (DTLA)
7.5
317 S Broadway, LA 90013.
A DTLA landmark since 1917.

Market Street Shopping District
4.5
100 N. Market St, Inglewood 90301

MARTIAL ARTS

See Capoeira, Tai Chi and Yoga for more information. Search the internet for Martial Arts near Crenshaw.

Bryan Hawkins Kenpo Karate
7.5 *12243 Venice Blvd, LA 90066.*

Kenji's Kajukenbo Academy
3.4 *1212 N. La Brea Ave., Inglewood 90302.*

Inosanto Academy of Martial Arts
8.3 *13352 Beach Ave, Marina Del Rey 90292.*

LA Judo Club
3.4 *3923 W Olympic Blvd, LA 90019.*

Moorimgoong Martial Arts
3.0 *1149 Crenshaw Blvd, LA 90019.*

MEAT

Best Buy Meat Co.
7108 S. Crenshaw Blvd., LA 90043.
0.0 Offering Chicken Sausage, Shrimp Sausage, Turkey Chops, Chicken and other poultry and meat options.

MEDITERRANEAN FOOD

See Egyptian Food, Greek Food, Halal, Hummus, Kabob, Palestinian and Restaurants for more.

Mizlala West Adams
2.6 *5400 W. Adams Blvd, LA 90016.*

📍 **Hummus House**
6.8 *12211 Hawthorne Blvd, Hawthorne 90250.*

📍 **Hummus Republic**
9.0 *709 N La Brea Ave, LA 90038.*

📍 **Quebobs Mediterranean Restaurant**
2.5 *3560 S La Cienega Blvd, Unit F, LA 90016.*

📍 **The Hummus Factory**
6.3 *6081 Center Dr, Unit 218, LA 90045.*

MEMORIALS

📍 **Dr. Martin Luther King Jr Civil Rights Memorial Tree Grove and Commemorative Obelisk**
3.9 *Kenneth Hahn State Recreation Area, 4100 S La Cienega Blvd, LA 90056.*
Dedicated to MLK Jr. The 15,000 sq. foot tree grove features an obelisk that evokes memories of the 1963 March on Washington for Jobs and Freedom.

📍 **El Pueblo de Los Angeles Historical Monument**
7.7 *125 Paseo De La Plaza, LA 90012.*

📍 **Jackie and Mack Robinson Memorial**
100 Garfield Ave, Pasadena 91101.
17.4 Outdoor sculpture of baseball player Jackie Robinson & his brother, Mack, an Olympic track athlete.

📍 **LA Memorial Coliseum**
3911 S Figueroa St, LA, 90037.
2.9 Home to the 1932, 1984 and 2022 Olympic Games.

📍 **Malcolm X Way**
4.6 *Central Ave and MLK Jr. Blvd.*

📍 **Mayor Tom Bradley Post Office**
3894 Crenshaw Blvd. LA 90008.
0.4 LA's first African American and longest serving Mayor.

📍 **Ray Charles Memorial Library**
3.6 *2107 W Washington Blvd, LA 90018.*

Walk a Mile in My Shoes Civil Rights Memorial

📍 Walk a Mile in My Shoes Civil Rights Memorial
1.0 #1 *Located at the corner of King and Obama.*

📍 Walk a Mile in My Shoes Civil Rights Memorial
1.9 #2 *Located at Jefferson and Obama Blvd.*

MEMORIAL PARKS

See Botanical Gardens, Cities and Neighborhoods, Destination Crenshaw, Gardens, Memorials and Commemorative Sites, Mercados, Public Art, and Walking Places for more information.

📍 **Biddy Mason Memorial Park**
333 S Spring St, LA 90013.
8.1 Featured in the park is *Biddy Mason Time and Place,* an 80-foot-long poured concrete wall by artist Sheila Levrant de Bretteville displaying a timeline of Biddy Mason's life and her freedom papers.

📍 **Ted Watkins Memorial Park**
6.0 *1335 E. 103rd St, LA 90002.*

MERCADO

See Markets for more information.

Mercado de la Paloma
3655 S Grand Ave, LA 90007.
3.9   Eight restaurants featuring cuisines ranging from
Ethiopian to Oaxacan, five artisanal shops, a coffee
shop and a couple of non-profits.

METRO BUS STOPS AND TRAIN STATIONS

Search LA METRO on the internet for more information.

MEXICAN FOOD

South LA is packed with Mexican food. See Restaurants for more
food, dining and restaurant-related options.

Cielito Lindo Restaurant
East 23 Olvera St, LA 90012.
8.3   Since 1934, CL has been serving taquitos, tamales &
burritos on historic Olvera Street - the oldest street in
LA. Google it to learn more.

El Cholo Mexican Restaurant

1.0 *1121 S Western Ave, LA 90006.*

1.9 *1037 S. Flower St. LA 90015.*

El Coyote Mexican Cafe
5.6 *7312 Beverly Blvd, LA 90036.*

El Paseo Inn Historic Landmark, Restaurant, Bar and Marketplace
8.3 *11 Olvera St, LA 90012.*
Features mural by artist Rubén Lara Campos.

Taqueria Los Anaya - Mexican Restaurant
4651 W Adams Blvd, LA 90016.
3.0 Taqueria Los Anaya specializes in authentic Mexican food, made with love and care.

MEXICO

The US/Mexico border is a short two to three hour drive from South LA.

Avenida Revolucion, Tijuana
Tijuana, Mexico.
142 Avenida Revolución is the tourist center in Tijuana, Baja California, México. It is a main thoroughfare of the historic downtown of Tijuana, officially called the Zona Centro.

Ensenada
Mexico, 22800.
207 Beach. Harbor. Nice waterfront. Nightlife.

La Bufadora
Mexico, 22800.
224 The second largest blowhole in the world, and the only one in North America.

Palacio de la Cultura de Tijuana
Calle Benito Juárez 2da Zona Centro Centro, 22000
142 *Tijuana, B.C., Mexico.*

Puerto Nuevo
147 Legendary lobster village.

Puerto Popotla
Small, quaint fishing village. Check it out before it's
165 gentrified.

Rosarito
Rosarito, Mexico 22710.
156 Famous beach town. Check out the Rosarito Beach Hotel.

Tijuana
Tijuana, Mexico.
142 Bustling border town.

MIRACLE MILE DISTRICT

Miracle Mile District
An LA neighborhood that runs along a stretch of
4.5 Wilshire Boulevard known as Museum Row.

MISSIONS

Both missions feature a garden, museum, gift shop and self-guided tours.

San Fernando Mission
22.9 *15151 San Fernando Mission Blvd, Mission Hills 91345.*
Founded on September 8, 1797.

San Gabriel Mission
19.3 *428 S Mission Dr, San Gabriel 91776.*
Founded in 1771.

MOVIE STUDIO TOURS

Paramount Pictures Studio Tour Hollywood
5.5 *5515 Melrose Ave, LA 90038.*

Sony Pictures Studio Tour
4.4 *10202 Washington Blvd, Culver City, 90232.*
A two-hour guided walking tour.

MOUNTAINS

Mount Baldy
53.0 *6778 Mt Baldy Rd, Mt Baldy 91759.*
Interpretive center, renovated 1920's schoolhouse, indoor nature trail, and a gift shop, and picnic tables.

San Bernardino Mountains
99.7 *CA 92305.*
The 11,503 foot San Gorgonio Mountain is the tallest peak in the range.

San Gabriel Mountains National Monument

43.4   *110 N Wabash Ave, Glendora 91741.*

MOUNT BALDY

See Cities and Neighborhoods Around South LA for more information.

MOVIE THEATERS

ArcLight Movie Theaters Culver City

4.2   *9500 Culver Blvd, Culver City 90232.*

ArcLight Movie Theaters Hollywood

6.8   *6360 Sunset Blvd, LA 90028.*

Blackout Cinema
Digital/cinematic space showcasing buried gems in black cinema.

Chinese Theater

7.3   *6925 Hollywood Blvd, Hollywood 90028.*

Cinemark Movie Theaters Baldwin Hills Crenshaw

0.2   *4020 Marlton Ave, LA 90008.*

Cinemark Movie Theaters at the Promenade

5.4   *6081 Center Dr, LA 90045.*

El Capitan Theatre

7.2   *6838 Hollywood Blvd, LA 90028.*

📍 **IMAX Movie Theater California Science Center**
3.5   *700 Exposition Park Dr, LA 90037.*

📍 **Regal 15 Cinemas Movie Theater - LA LIVE**
6.1   *1000 W Olympic Blvd, LA 90015.*

📍 **The Egyptian Movie Theatre**
7.2   *6712 Hollywood Blvd. Hollywood, 90028.*

MURALS

Check out Social and Public Art Resource Center to find more.

📍 **America Tropical**
Olvera St, LA 90012.
8.3   By David Alfaro Siqueiros.

📍 **Black Seed (1990)**
2301 W. Jefferson Blvd, LA 90018.
1.9   By Eddie Orr, David Mosley and William T. Stubbs.

📍 **Cecil (1998/1999)**
1727 East 107th Street, Watts 90002.
10.3   By Richard Wyatt.

📍 **City of Dreams / River of History**
811 N. Vignes St, LA 90012.
8.5   By Richard Wyatt.

📍 **The Great Wall of Crenshaw**
Crenshaw Blvd at 50th St.
1.5   Painted by graffiti collective Rocking The Nation.

Freedom Won't Wait (1992)
2.7
1815 W 54th St., LA 90062.
By Artist Noni Olabisi.

Heart of Hyde Park
0.8
5726 Crenshaw, LA 90043.
By Moses Ball and LA Commons.

Kobe Bryant Mural (2020)
6.0
1336 Lebanon St, LA 90015.
Search Kobe Bryant murals to find more.

Love is For Everyone (1990)
1.7
5149 West Jefferson Blvd, LA 90016.
By Mary Linn-Hughes and Reginald Zachary. On side of the Minority AIDS Project building.

Nipsey Hussle
1.7
LA 90043. (Near Crenshaw Blvd and Slauson.)
Located near the intersection of Crenshaw Blvd and Slauson.

The Elixir
0.3
Near Crenshaw Blvd and Stocker.
Painted by Patrick Henry Johnson. Located just south of the intersection of Crenshaw Blvd and Stocker.

The History of Transportation (1942)
4.7
101 E Kelso St, Inglewood 90301.
By Helen Lundeberg. The largest petrachrome mural in the world.

The Last Stand = Unite (2001)
0.7
4331 Degnan Blvd, LA 90008.
By Carla Carr. Located in the alley on the south side of Hot and Cool Cafe.

The Resurrection of Watts (2001)
10950 South Central Ave, LA 90059.
9.7 By Ras Ammar Nsoroma.

To Protect and Serve (1992)
3406 11th Avenue, LA 90018.
1.4 By Artist Noni Olabisi.

Troubled Island (2003)
2520 W View Street, LA 90016.
2.1 By Artist Noni Olabisi.

Visions and Motions (1992)
4828 Crenshaw Blvd, LA 90043.
1.8 By Elliot Pickney. On the side of the Community Youth Sports & Arts Foundation.

Women Do Get Weary But They Don't Give Up (1990)
3720 West 54th, LA 90043.
1.5 By Alice Patrick.

Young People of Watts
10712 Wilmington Ave., Watts.
10.4 By Christena Cardenas.

MUSEUMS

Being the world-class city that it is, LA is full of museums. Here's a few worth checking out.

African American Firefighter Museum
7.6 *1401 S Central Ave, LA 90021.*

Art + Practice - Art Gallery Museum
0.7   *4339 Leimert Blvd., LA 90008.*

Autry Museum of the American West
12.1   *4700 Western Heritage Way, LA 90027.*

Avila Adobe Firehouse Museum
7.7   *501 N. Los Angeles St, LA 90012.*

California African American Museum
3.0   *600 State Dr. LA 90037.*

California Jazz and Blues Museum
0.7   *4317 Degnan Blvd, LA 90008.*

California Science Center Museum
3.0   *700 Exposition Park Dr. LA 90037.*

Cayton's Children Museum
11.5   *395 Santa Monica Place, Santa Monica, 90401.*

Centinela Adobe Museum
5.8   *7634 Midfield Ave, LA 90045.*

Chinese American Museum
8.1   *425 N LA St, LA 90012.*

Destination Crenshaw Open-Air Museum (Planned)
1.1   Open-air public art space.   Crenshaw Blvd between Vernon and Slauson.

Dominguez Rancho Adobe Museum
18.2   *18127 S. Alameda St, Compton 90220.*

El Pueblo de Los Angeles Historical Monument + Museums
7.7 *125 Paseo De La Plaza, LA, 90012.*

Grammy Museum
6.3 *800 W Olympic Blvd, LA 90015.*

Hidden History Museum
5.2 *2131 W. Jefferson Blvd., LA 90018.*

Japanese American National Museum
7.7 *100 N Central Ave, LA 90012.*

La Brea Tar Pits and Museum
5.2 *5801 Wilshire Blvd, LA 90036.*

Los Angeles County Museum of Art
5905 Wilshire Blvd, LA 90036.
5.5 The largest art museum in the western US.

Lucas Museum of Narrative Art (Planned)
2.7 *Exposition Park, LA 90007.*

Museum of African American Art Los Angeles
0.1 *4005 Crenshaw Blvd, LA 90008.*

Museum of Tolerance
6.2 *9786 Pico Blvd, LA 90035.*

Natural History Museum of LA County
900 W Exposition Blvd, LA 90007.
3.0 The largest natural and historical museum in the western US.

Pio Pico Adobe Museum and State Historic Park
23.7 *6003 Pioneer Blvd, Whittier 90606.*

Rancho Los Cerritos Historic Site & Museum
21.2 *4600 Virginia Rd, Long Beach 90807.*

Space Shuttle Museum
700 Exposition Park Dr, LA 90037.
3.0
Space Shuttle Endeavour is a retired orbiter from NASA's Space Shuttle program and the fifth and final operational shuttle built.

Tomorrow's Aeronautical Museum
961 W. Alondra Blvd, Compton 90220.
13.4
At Compton Airport.

N

NATURE CENTER

⦿ **Stoneview Nature Center and Demonstration Garden**
3.0
5950 Stoneview Dr. Culver City, 90232.
Urban sanctuary nestled in the Western Baldwin Hills with scenic views of the Santa Monica.

NATURE MUSEUMS

⦿ **Augustus Hawkins Wetlands Nature Museum**
6.5 *5790 Compton Ave., LA 90011.*

⦿ **Ferndell Nature Museum**
13.7 *2800 E Observatory Rd, LA 90027.*

NATURE PARKS

See Arboretums, Art Walks, Beaches, Bike Paths, Caves, Exercise, Hiking Trails, Lakes, Walking Paths, Wetlands, and Wildlife Reserves, etc. for more information about walking paths and hiking trails.

⦿ **Augustus Hawkins Nature Park + Wetlands**
6.5 *5790 Compton Ave., LA 90011.*

Compton Creek Natural Park

941 W Cressey St, Compton 90222.

12.9 Featuring natural habitat, walking paths, grassy areas, fitness equipment, picnic areas, amphitheater, parking, plaza, and interpretive signage.

Marsh Street Nature Park

2944 Gleneden St, LA 90039.

12.9 Over 100 trees, native plants, birds, bees and butterflies. Aka, MacAdams Riverfront Park.

NEWSPAPERS

Los Angeles Sentinel/LA Watts Times

3800 Crenshaw Blvd, LA 90008.

0.6 African American owned and operated.

Our Weekly LA Newspaper

8732 S Western Ave, LA 90047.

5.0 Provides coverage relevant to African-American readers.

La Opinion

The largest Spanish-language newspaper in the US.

Los Angeles Standard Newspaper (LASN)

Covers South LA's African/Back communities.

NIGHTCLUBS

See Entertainment Centers for more information.

Catch One Nightclub (CON)
2.9 *4067 Pico Blvd, LA 90019.*

El Floridita Latin/Salsa Nightclub
6.2 *1253 Vine St, LA 90038.*

Fais Do Do Cafe Nightclub
2.3 *5257 W Adams Blvd, LA 90016.*

Regency West
3339 W. 43rd St., LA 90008.
0.6 Banquet Hall and local gathering spot.

Savoy Entertainment Center Nightclub
4.8 *218 South La Brea Ave, Inglewood 90301.*

Mayan Nightclub
6.5 *1038 S Hill St, LA 90015.*

The New Townhouse LA Restaurant + Nightclub
6835 La Tijera Blvd, LA 90045.
4.4 Entertainment and fine dining featuring Southern Cuisine.

O

OBAMA

📍 **President Barack Obama Blvd**
0.8 *Runs between La Cienega Blvd and Western Ave.*

OBSERVATORY

📍 **Griffith Scientific Observatory Museum**
2800 E Observatory Rd, LA 90027.
10.1 Look at stars, visit the Samuel Oschin Planetarium, explore the exhibits, and enjoy scenic views of LA.

OCEAN

Refer to Beaches for more information.

📍 **Pacific Ocean**
22 miles of Pacific Ocean coastline. Numerous beach
10.0 cities and hundreds of things to do including counting grains of sand.

OCEANSIDE

See Cities and Neighborhoods Around South LA for more information.

OLVERA STREET

See Museums for El Pueblo de Los Angeles Historical Monument to learn more.

Olvera Street

7.7 LA's first street and home of the oldest standing residence in LA's.

P

PALESTINIAN FOOD

See Restaurants for more food, dining and restaurant-related options.

Jerusalem Chicken
2.6 *4448 W Slauson, LA 90043.*
A Palestinian Chicken Eatery.

PALM TREES

Check out South LA's iconic Palm trees

Historic Palm Tree of Los Angeles
3.3 *500 Exposition Park Dr, LA 90037.*
Read the marker describing the oldest palm tree in the city.

Iconic South LA Palm Tree Lined Avenues:

0.7 *Obama Blvd between Crenshaw Blvd and La Brea Ave.*

1.4 *11th Ave between Vernon Ave and 48th St.*

PARKS

See also Art Parks, Nature Parks, Recreation Centers, Skate Parks, Wetlands, etc. for more information.

Athens Park
9.9 *12603 S Broadway, LA 90061.*

Central Park
5.4 *1357 E. 22nd St., LA 90011.*

Dr. Martin Luther King Jr Park
1.7 *3916 South Western Ave., LA 90062.*

East Rancho Dominguez Park
17.1 *15116 S. Atlantic Ave, Compton 90221.*

Edward Vincent Jr. Park
3.2 *700 Warren Ln, Inglewood, 90302.*

Eleanor Green Roberts Park
2.9 *4526 W Pico Blvd, LA 90019.*

Exposition Park
701 State Dr, LA 90037.
3.6 Seven acre garden surrounded by seven world-class museums and an IMAX theater.

Green Meadows Park
7.6 *431 E 89th St, LA 90003.*

Helen Keller Park
8.7 *12521 S. Vermont Ave. LA 90044.*

Hemingway Park
13.2 *16605 San Pedro St, Carson 90746.*

Jesse Owens Park

5.7 *9835 S Western Ave, LA 90047.*
Indoor swimming pool, outdoor basketball courts, golf course.

Kenneth Hahn State Park

2.4 *4100 S La Cienega Blvd, LA 90056.*

Norman O. Houston Park

2.3 *4800 S. La Brea, LA 90008.*
Walking path lined with fitness equipment.

Rueben Ingold Park

2.0 *4400 W Mt Vernon Dr, View Park 90043.*
Surfaced walkway and workout equipment.

Tongva Park

11.4 *1615 Ocean Ave, Santa Monica, 90401.*
Ocean views.

PASTRAMI

Johnny's Pastrami

1.6 *4327 W Adams Blvd, LA 90007.*

PEANUTS

NE Conaway Peanuts

0.6 *3818 Crenshaw Blvd, LA 90008.*
South LA's best roasted peanuts.

PERFORMING ARTS

Barbara Morrison Performing Arts Center
0.6 *4305 Degnan Blvd, LA 90008.*

Bob Baker Marionette Theater
11.4 *4949 York Blvd, LA 90042.*
LA's oldest children's theater company.

Nate Holden Performing Arts Center & Ebony Repertory Theater
2.6 *4708 W Washington Blvd, LA 90016.*

World Stage Performance Gallery
0.8 *4344 Degnan Blvd, LA 90008.*

PETTING ZOOS

See Wetlands, Wildlife and Zoos for more information.

Griffith Park Pony Rides & Petting Zoo
10.5 *4400 Crystal Springs Dr, LA 90027.*

PHOTOGRAPHY

Venice Arts Center for Photography & Film Education
7.8 *13445 Beach Ave, Marina Del Rey 90292.*

PIERS

◯ **Manhattan Beach Pier**
11.5 *Manhattan Beach, 90266.*

◯ **Pelican Pier**
17.1 *411 Shoreline Village Dr, Long Beach 90802.*

◯ **Redondo Beach Pier**
14.0 *Redondo Beach 90277.*

◯ **Santa Monica Pier**
11.7 *Santa Monica 90401.*

◯ **Venice Beach Pier**
9.3 *Venice 90291.*

PIZZA

See Restaurants for more food, dining and restaurant-related options.

 Delicious Vinyl Pizza Restaurant
2.8 *5419 W Adams Blvd, LA 90016.*

PLANETARIUM

 Samuel Oschin Planetarium
      2800 E Observatory Rd, LA 90027.
10.1 Visitors can look through a telescope, see a live show
      iexplore the exhibits, and enjoy the spectacular views
      of LA and the Hollywood Sign.

PLAYA DEL REY

See Cities and Neighborhoods Around South LA for more information.

PLAZAS

Chinatown Central Plaza
8.9
943 N Broadway, LA 90012.
See the East Gate, Golden Pagoda, and make a wish at the Seven Star Cavern Wishing Well.

Gilbert Lindsey Plaza
5.7
1201 Figueroa Dr, LA 90015.
Located on the corner of Figueroa and Pico.

Japanese Village Plaza
8.2
335 E. 2nd Street, LA 90012.
Gateway to Little Tokyo.

La Placita (The Little Plaza)
7.7
125 Paseo De La Plaza, LA 90012.
Celebrate's LA's birthplace.

Leimert Park Village Plaza
1.0
4395 Leimert Blvd., LA 90008.

PRESERVES

See Reserves or more information.

Briar Summit Open Space Preserve
10.4
LA 90046.

Ferndell Nature Preserve
5375 Red Oak Dr, LA 90068.
13.7   Tropical foliage. Man-made brook. 50 fern species.

Forrestal Nature Preserve
155-acre, beachfront with hiking trails, picturesque
27.9   lookouts & native animals.

Mt. Baldy Wilderness Preserve
Barrett Stoddard Truck Trail, Claremont 91711.
52.1   Scenic vistas and habitat preservation.

Verdugo Mountains Open Space Preserve
Oakmount View Dr, Glendale 91209.
23.0   Biking & horseback riding.

PUBLIC ART

See Memorials, Monuments, Murals, Museums, Sculpture
Gardens, Statues and Watts Towers or search for Public Art in
Public Places; the LA County Arts and Culture webpage; Civic Arts
and/or Inglewood Public Art for more information.

Blue Line Oasis
1920 S Acacia Ave, Compton 90220.
15.7   By Lynn Aldrich. Blue line station.

Compton Past, Present and Future
275 N Willowbrook Ave, Compton 90220.
14.6   By Eva Cockcroft. Blue line station.

Dominguez Field and The Famous Titans of Aviation
Atlantic Ave, East Compton 90221.
17.1   By Fausto Fernandez.

Endless Miles

12021 Wilmington Ave, LA 90059.

11.4 By Rob Ley. At MLK Jr Medical Campus.

Locus City Imprints

11500 S Figueroa St, LA 90061.

6.3 By Steve Appleton. Blue Line Harbor Freeway Station.

Rise and Shine (2017)

150 E El Segundo Blvd, LA 90061.

10.5 By Greenmeme. In A.C. Bilbrew Library.

The Triforium (1975)

Fletcher Bowron Square, LA 90012.

8.3 A 60-foot high, concrete public art sculpture mounted with 1,494 Venetian glass prisms, light bulbs, and an internal 79-bell carillon. By Joseph Young.

Urban Light

5905 Wilshire Blvd, LA 90036.

5.5 By Chris Burden. Located at LACMA.

What Wall (1998)

3524 Hayden Ave, Culver City 90232.

3.2 By Architect Eric Owen Moss for Culver City's Architecture as Art program.

Woodside Mural (2014)

8970 Washington Blvd, Culver City 90232.

3.9 By Jason Woodside.

PUMPKINS

Mr. Bones Pumpkin Patch
10100 Jefferson Blvd., Culver City 90232.

3.7

Brings the farm to the city and celebrates the magic of Halloween.

Q

QUEENS

Queen Anne Recreation Center
3.1 *1240 West Blvd, LA 90019.*

Queen Mary Hotel Long Beach
24.5 *1126 Queens Hwy, Long Beach 90802.*

Queen Park Learning Garden
3.8 *652 E. Queen St, Inglewood 90301.*

Queen of Sheba Ethiopian Restaurant
3.1 *630 N. La Brea #106, Inglewood 90302.*

R

RADIO PROGRAMS

There are many radio stations/music programs to choose from in South LA. These focus on blues, hip-hop, jazz, salsa, samba and soul.

Alma del Barrio Latin Music Radio Program (KXLU 88.9)
Salsa & Latin music. Weekends 6 am to 6 pm.

Brazilian Hour Radio Program (KXLU 88.9)
Brazilian music. Weekends from 9 am to 10 am.

Jazz (KJAZZ 88.1)
America's only 24/7 Jazz station.

Jazz on the Latin Side (KJAZZ 88.1)
Friday's 8 pm to 11 pm. Saturday's 6 pm to 10 pm.

Kindness, Joy, Love and Happiness (KJLH 102.3 FM)
161 N La Brea Ave, Inglewood, 90301.
Contemporary R&B 24/7. Owned by Stevie Wonder.

Nothing But the Blues (KJAZZ 88.1)
Blues music. Saturday's 2 pm until 6:00 pm, Sunday's from 2 pm till 7 pm. Hosted by Gary Wagner.

Rhapsody in Black (KPFK 90.7)
Classic R&B from the 40's thru the 70's. Hosted by "Big Daddy Bill" Gardner.

RECREATION CENTERS

Franklin D. Roosevelt Park Recreation Center
6.0 *7600 Graham Ave, LA 90001.*

Hansen Dam Recreation Center
30.5 *11798 Foothill Blvd, Lake View Terrace 91342.*

Jim Gilliam Recreation Center
1.5 *4000 South La Brea Ave, LA 90008.*

Kenneth Hahn State Recreation Area
3.2 *4100 S. La Cienega Blvd, LA 90056.*

Ladera Park Recreation Center
2.7 *6027 Ladera Park Ave, LA 90056.*

Loren Miller Recreation Center
3.2 *2717 S Halldale Ave, LA 90018.*

Earvin Magic Johnson Recreation Area
10.9 *1050 E 120th St, LA 90059.*

Oakwood Park Recreation Center
9.4 *767 California Ave, Venice, 90291.*

Palisades Park Recreation Center
14.8 *851 Alma Real Dr, Pacific Palisades 90272.*

Rancho Cienega Recreation Center
1.3 *5001 Rodeo Rd, LA, 90016.*

Roy A. Anderson Recreation Center
2.6 *3980 Bill Robertson Lane, LA, 90037.*

South Park Recreation Center (aka Barry White Park)
4.8   *345 E. 51st St, LA 90011.*

St. Andrews Recreation Center
4.8   *8701 S St Andrews Pl, LA 90047.*

Van Ness Recreation Center
2.2   *5720 2nd Ave, LA 90043.*

Venice Beach Recreation Center
9.4   *1800 Ocean Front Walk, Venice 90291.*

REDONDO BEACH

See Cities and Neighborhoods Around South LA for more information.

REGGAE MUSIC

Google "reggae music in LA" to find many places to get your groove on.

Dub Club - Reggae Night
8.7   *1154 Glendale Blvd, LA 90026.*
Weekly Wednesday night's at the Echoplex.

RESERVES

See Arboretums, Art Walks, Beaches, Bike Paths, Caves, Exercise, and Hiking Trails, Lakes, Nature Parks and Preserves, Reservoirs, Walking Paths,Wetlands, and Wildlife Reserves, etc,... for more information about walking paths and hiking trails.

Hollywood Reservoir
8.9
LA 90068.
Three mile path. Views of Hollywood Sign.

Morningside Park Reservoir
4.1
Inglewood 90305.

Silver Lake Reservoir
11.1
LA 90039.

RESTAURANTS

See also Bakeries, Bar-B-Que, Cajun and Creole, Cafe's and Coffee, French Dip Sandwiches, Fried Chicken, Greek Food, Health Food, Halal Cuisine, Hot Dogs, Hummus, Jamaican Food, Japanese Food, Kebab, Korean Food, Mexican Food, Pizza, Sandwiches, Soul Food, Steak Houses, Tacos and Vegan/Vegetarian for more information.

Ackee Bamboo Jamaican Restaurant
0.5
4305 Degnan Blvd, LA 90008.

Alta Adams "Soul Food"
2.6
5359 W Adams Blvd, LA 90016.

Azla Ethiopian Vegan Cuisine
0.5
4309 Leimert Blvd, LA 90008.

Baba's Vegan Cafe
3.6   *6619 S. Western Ave, LA 90047.*

Bludso's Bar & Que
6.6   *609 N La Brea Ave, LA 90036.*

Cielito Lindo Restaurant
8.3   *E. 23 Olvera St, LA 90012.*

Cole's French Dip Restaurant and Bar
7.1   *118 E 6th St, LA 90014.*

Delicious Southern Cuisine:

4371 Crenshaw Blvd, LA 90008.
0.7

4229 S. Central Ave, LA 90011.
4.9   At The Historic Dunbar Hotel.

Delicious Vinyl Pizza Restaurant
2.8   *5419 W Adams Blvd, LA 90016.*

Dinah's Diner
5.5   *6521 S. Sepulveda Blvd, LA 90045.*

Dulan's Soul Food Restaurants:

202 E Manchester Blvd, Inglewood 90301.
4.5

4859 Crenshaw Blvd, LA 90043.
1.1

Earle's Grill Restaurant
0.5   *3864 Crenshaw Blvd, LA 90008.*

El Cholo Mexican Restaurant:

📍 *1121 S Western Ave, LA 90006.*
4.1

📍 *1037 S. Flower St. LA 90015.*
6.7

📍 **El Coyote Mexican Cafe**
5.6 *7312 Beverly Blvd, LA 90036.*

📍 **El Paseo Inn Historic Landmark, Restaurant, Bar and Marketplace**
8.3 *11 Olvera St, LA 90012.*
Features mural painted by Rubén Lara Campos.

📍 **Fleming's Prime Steakhouse & Wine Bar**
5.9 *800 W Olympic Blvd, LA 90015.*

📍 **Floridita Restaurant**
1253 Vine St, LA 90038.
6.2 Cuban and Caribbean cuisine.

📍 **Fogo de Chao Brazilian Steakhouse**
4.9 *800 S Figueroa St, LA 90017.*

📍 **Gus's World Famous Fried Chicken**
2.8 *1262 Crenshaw Blvd, LA 90019.*

📍 **Harold and Belle's New Orleans Restaurant & Loung**
1.5 *2920 W. Jefferson Blvd, LA 90018.*

📍 **Honey Bee's House of Breakfast**
1.8 *4715 W Adams Blvd, LA 90016.*

Jeang Yuk Jeom Korean BB
4.5 *621 S Western Ave #100, LA 90005.*

Kang Nam - Traditional Korean Restaurant
3.4 *4103 W Olympic Blvd, LA 90019.*

La Louisianne Cajun Creole Soul Food Restaurant
2.6 *5812 Overhill Dr, LA 90043.*

Lavender Blue Restaurant Lounge
4.4 *3310 W. Manchester Blvd. Inglewood, 90305.*

Marilyn's Soul Food
1.5 *2638 Crenshaw Blvd, LA 90016.*

Mercado De Paloma Restaurant Food Court
3.9 *3655 S Grand Ave, LA 90007.*

Mike's Deli Sandwich Shop Restaurant
3.0 *4859 W. Slauson Ave., LA 90056.*

Mizlala West Adams
2.6 *5400 West Adams Blvd, LA 90016.*

Morton's the Steakhouse
5.9 *435 S. La Cienega Blvd. LA 90048.*

Musso and Frank Steakhouse Grill
7.2 *6667 Hollywood Blvd, Hollywood, 90028.*

Natraliart Jamaican Restaurant
2.7 *3426 W. Washington Blvd, LA 90018.*

Papa Christo's Greek Restaurant, Deli and Taverna
4.5 *2771 Pico Blvd, LA 90006.*

Philippe's Restaurant - The Original French Dip
8.5   *1001 North Alameda, LA 90012.*

Pink's Hot Dogs
6.0   *709 N La Brea Ave, LA 90038.*

Redondo Beach Fish Market
14.0   *123 Intl. Boardwalk, Redondo Beach 90277.*

Restaurant Row Beverly Hills
7.0   *La Cienega Blvd between Wilshire and San Vicente.*

Roscoe's House of Chicken and Waffles
7.1   Multiple locations.   See Fried Chicken for more information.

Shaquille's Southern Cuisine
6.3   *800 W Olympic Blvd, LA 90015.*

Simply Wholesome Health Food Restaurant & Store
2.6   *4508 W Slauson Ave, LA 90043.*

Sizzler Steak House:

   831 E Manchester Blvd, Inglewood 90301.
4.3

   5801 Sepulveda Blvd, Culver City 90230.
4.8

Sweet Chick's Fried Chicken
6.4   *448 N Fairfax Ave, LA 90036.*

Swift Vegan Cafe
0.5   *4279 Crenshaw Blvd, LA 90008.*

Taylor's Steak House
4.6   *3361 W 8th St, LA 90005.*

Taqueria Los Anaya
3.0   *4651 W. Adams Blvd, LA 90016.*

The Cork Bar and Grill
1.9   *4771 W. Adams Blvd, LA 90016.*

The District Restaurant and Bar
0.3   *3888 Crenshaw Blvd, LA 90008.*

The Nile Restaurant and Bar
0.5   *207 S Market St, Inglewood 90301.*

Versailles Cuban Restaurant:

4.5   *10319 Venice Blvd, LA 90034.*

4.7   *1415 S La Cienega Blvd, LA 90035.*

Worldwide Tacos
1.0   *2419 W King Blvd, LA 90008.*

Yamashiro's
7.7   *1999 N. Sycamore Ave, LA 90068.*
Pan-Asian food.

RIVERS AND CREEKS

Ballona Creek
3.5 Starts in Culver City. Runs 9 miles from Baldwin Hills to the Pacific Ocean.

Los Angeles River
9.0 The 51-mile river flows through Compton and Long Beach.

LA River Center & Gardens and the Mountains Recreation & Conservation Authority
10.1 *570 W Ave 26 #100, LA 90065.*

Rio Hondo River
Irwindale 91010.
28.4 An LA River tributary. Starts near Whittier Narrows.

San Gabriel River Watershed
39.7 Flows 58 miles southward from the San Gabriel Dam to the Pacific Ocean.

ROSE GARDEN

See Arboretums, Art Parks, Botanical, Chinese, Japanese and Sculpture Gardens, Nature Parks and Preserves, Wetlands and Wildlife Refuges, etc for more garden-related information.

Exposition Park Rose Garden
701 State Dr, LA 90037.
3.6 Seven acre garden surrounded by museums.

RUNNING CLUBS

Leimert Park Running Club
0.8   Meets Saturday mornings at Grayburn Ave and
       Coliseum St.

S

SALSA MUSIC AND DANCE

There are a lot of places to listen and dance to salsa music in South LA.

Alma del Barrio Latin Music Radio Program (KXLU 88.9)
Salsa & Latin music. Weekends 6 am to 6 pm.

DTLA Salsa Festival
7.1
532 S. Olive St., LA 90013.
Annual July event. Sponsored by the LA Department of Cultural Affairs. Held in Pershing Square.

El Floridita Restaurant and Nightclub
6.2
1253 Vine St, LA, CA 90038.
Live salsa music, dinner and dancing.

Jazz on the Latin Side (KJAZZ 88.1)
Friday's 8 pm to 11 pm. Saturday's 6 pm to 10 pm.

La Plaza de Cultura y Artes
6.2
501 N. Main St., LA 90012.
Salsa and Latin music events throughout the year. Check their website.

Salsa At The Shaw
0.2
3650 W. MLK Jr. Blvd., LA 90008.
At the Crenshaw Plaza Farmers Market 10 am to 3 pm. Last Saturday of the month.

The Mayan Theater and Night Club
1038 S Hill St, LA 90015.
6.5
Formerly a landmark movie palace, currently a nightclub and music venue.

SAN DIEGO

See Cities and Neighborhoods Around South LA for more information.

SANDWICH SHOPPES

Mikes Deli Sandwich Shop Restaurant
4859 W. Slauson Ave., LA 90056.
3.0
Offers a wide variety of classic subs and sandwiches made to order in hearty portions.

Orleans and York Deli:

400 E Florence Ave Inglewood 90301.
0.4

3868 Crenshaw Blvd LA 90008.
2.7

4454 W Slauson Ave, Windsor Hills 90043.
4.0

SANTA CLAUS

Ho, Ho, Ho, ethnic Santa's.

Black Santa
0.1 Baldwin Hills Crenshaw Mall

Shogun Santa
8.2 Japanese Village in Little Tokyo.

SANTA MONICA

See Cities and Neighborhoods Around South LA for more information.

SCULPTURE GARDENS

See Museums and Public Art to find more information about Sculpture in South LA. See Arboretums, Art Parks, Art Walks, Beaches, Bike Paths, Caves, Exercise, Gardens, Hiking Trails, Lakes, Nature Parks and Preserves, Reservoirs, Walking Paths, Wetlands, and Wildlife Reserves for more information about walking paths and hiking trails.

B. Gerald Cantor Sculpture Garden
5.2 *5905 Wilshire Blvd. LA 90036.*

Cerritos Sculpture Garden
25.0 *183rd St, Cerritos 90703.*

Franklin D Murphy Sculpture Garden
10.0 *245 Charles E Young Dr E, LA, CA 90095.*

📍 **Hollywood Sculpture Garden**
8.1 *2430 Vasanta Way, LA 90068.*

📍 **Museum of Latin American Art Sculpture Garden**
24.2 *628 Alamitos Ave, Long Beach 90802.*

📍 **The Fran and Ray Stark Sculpture Garden and the Central Garden**
13.6 *1200 Getty Center Drive, LA 90049.*

SENIOR CITIZENS CENTERS

Senior citizen centers offer activities, programs, and special events.

📍 **Ahmanson Senior Citizen Center**
2.6 *3990 Bill Robertson Ln, LA 90037.*

📍 **Culver City Senior Center**
4.6 *095 Overland Ave, Culver City 90232.*

📍 **Inglewood Senior Citizens Center**
3.8 *330 Centinela Ave, Inglewood 90302.*

📍 **Watts Senior Citizens Center**
9.8 *1657 E Century Blvd, LA 90002.*

📍 **Westchester Senior Center**
7.6 *8740 Lincoln Blvd, LA 90045.*

📍 **Yvonne B. Burke Senior Community Center**
3.0 *4750 W 62nd St, LA 90056.*

SHOE REPAIR

Gilbee's Shoe Repair
0.4   3870 Crenshaw Blvd #104, LA 90008.

SHOPPING AND SHOPPING MALLS

See Cities and Neighborhoods Around South LA, Festivals, Mercados, and Markets for more information.

Baldwin Hills Crenshaw Plaza Mall
0.1   *3650 W. King Blvd, LA 90008.*

Beverly Center Shopping Mall
6.3   *8500 Beverly Blvd, LA 90048.*

LA Fashion District
6.8   Off 11 St between Los Angeles Street and San Pedro Street.

Fox Hills Mall
4.5   *6000 Sepulveda Blvd, Culver City 90230.*

Japanese Village Plaza
8.2   *335 E. 2nd Street.*

Market Street Shopping District
4.5   *100 N. Market St, Inglewood 90301.*
Inglewood's Market Street district has art galleries, book stores, the Inglewood Senior Center and the light rail Florence Boulevard station.

Mercado la Paloma
3.9   *3655 S Grand Ave, LA 90007.*

Rodeo Drive

7.4 Expensive world-famous shopping and dining. Between Wilshire Blvd and Santa Monica Blvd.

Santee Alley Shopping

6.4 *210 E Olympic Blvd, LA 90015.*

The Grove

189 The Grove Dr, LA 90036.

5.6 Very cool mall, next to the historical farmers market, a popular fashion and lifestyle destination offering a mix of retail, restaurants and entertainment.

SKATE PARKS

Boards and Wheels: Rock, skate, roll, bounce. Get your Roller Skatin' on in Crenshaw. Public skateboarding park with street-inspired features such as stairs, ledges, railings & ramps.

Charmette Bonpua Skate Plaza Park

1.2 *5001 Rodeo Rd, LA 90016.*

Culver City Skate Park

3.5 *9910 Jefferson Blvd, Culver City 90232.*

Darby Park SkateBoard Area

3400 W Arbor Vitae St, Inglewood 90305.

4.6 Park has playground & areas for picnics, tennis, basketball, skateboards & field sports.

Eucalyptus Skate Park

7.4 *12100 S. Inglewood Ave. Hawthorne 90250.*

Gilbert Lindsay Skate Park

4.9 *429 E. 42nd Place, LA 90011.*

Venice Skate Park

10.1
800 Ocean Front Walk, Venice 90291.
Oceanfront skatepark featuring a sunken pool & a
street-inspired area with stairs, ledges & rails.

SKATE SHOP

Neighbors Skate Shop

0.7 *4344 Degnan Blvd, LA 90008.*

SKID ROW

See Cities and Neighborhoods Around South LA for more
information.

SLOT CAR RACING

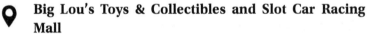

**Big Lou's Toys & Collectibles and Slot Car Racing
Mall**

5.0
5413 Sepulveda Blvd, Culver City 90230.
Spacious shop packed with toys & collectibles, plus a
slot-car track for racing events.

SNOW-RELATED ACTIVITIES

Like Skiing, Sliding and Sledding?

Big Bear Mountain Resort

109 *880 Summit Blvd, Big Bear Lake, CA 92315.*

Mount Baldy Ski Resort
57.5 *8401 Mt Baldy Rd, Mt Baldy 91759.*

Mountain High Resorts
88.8 *24510 CA-2, Wrightwood, CA 92397.*

Snow Summit Mountain Resort
107 *880 Summit Blvd, Big Bear Lake, CA 92315.*

SOUL FOOD

Alta Adams "Soul Food"
2.6 *5359 W Adams Blvd, LA 90016.*

Delicious Southern Cuisine

4371 Crenshaw Blvd, LA 90008.
0.7

Delicious Southern Cuisine
4.9 At The Historic Dunbar Hotel

Dulan's Soul Food Restaurants:

202 E Manchester Blvd, Inglewood 90301.
4.5

4859 Crenshaw Blvd, LA 90043.
1.1

Granny's Kitchen Southern Style Soul Food
5.7 *5440 S Central Ave, LA 90011.*

Marilyn's Soul Food
1.5 *2638 Crenshaw Blvd, LA 90016.*
Classic, affordable soul food.

My Two Cents LA
4.2 *5583 W Pico Blvd, LA 90019.*

SPORTFISHING

See Fishing for more fish-related information.

Marina del Rey Sportfishing
8.4 *13759 Fiji Way, Marina Del Rey, CA 90292.*

Redondo Beach Sportfishing
14.7 *140 Intl. Boardwalk, Redondo Beach 90277.*

SPORT STADIUMS

BMO Stadium
3.0 *3939 S. Figueroa Ave, LA 90037.*
Home of the LA Football Club.

Dignity Health Sports Park
15.0 *18400 S Avalon, Carson 90746.*

Dodger Stadium
9.4 *1000 Vin Scully Ave, LA 90012.*

LA Memorial Coliseum
2.9 *3911 S Figueroa St, LA, 90037.*
Home to the 1932, 1984 and 2022 Olympic Games.

📍 **Rose Bowl Stadium**
17.7 *1001 Rose Bowl Dr, Pasadena, CA 91103.*

📍 **Staples Center**
6.1 *1111 S Figueroa St, LA 90015.*
Music, sports and entertainment center, right in the heart of LA.

📍 **So-Fi Stadium and Entertainment District at Hollywood Park**
5.8 *3883 W Century Blvd, Inglewood 90303.*
Home of the LA Rams and the LA Chargers.

SPRINGS

See Aquatic Centers, Beaches, Lakes, and Wetlands for more water-related information.

📍 **Centinela Springs**
3.2 *700 Warren Ln, Inglewood, 90302.*
Bubbling springs once flowed here from their source in a deep water basin that has existed continuously since the Pleistocene Era. California Historical Landmark #363. Inside Edward Vincent Park.

SQUARES

See Botanical Gardens Cities and Neighborhoods, Destination Crenshaw, Gardens, Memorials and Commemorative Sites, Memorial Parks, Mercados, Public Art, and Walking Places for more information.

📍 **Archbishop Carl Bean Square**

1.8 *Corner of W. Jefferson Blvd. and S. Sycamore Ave, 90016.* Dedicated to the founder of the Minority AIDS Project and the Unity Fellowship Church Movement, America's first affirming and welcoming Black church for the LGBTQ community.

📍 **Crenshaw Square**

0.4 *3870 Crenshaw Blvd, LA 90008.* Dining. Restaurant & Bar. Shopping. Hair. Nails. Shoes. Etc.

📍 **Iman Hasan Square**

4.5 *Corner of Central Ave and MLK Jr Blvd.*

📍 **Mayor Tom Bradley Square**

0.4 *3894 Crenshaw Blvd., LA 90008.* Honors the 38th Mayor of Los Angeles serving from 1973 to 1993.

📍 **Nipsey Hussle Square**

2.2 *Intersection of Crenshaw and Slauson. 90043.* Honors the vision of Nipsey Hussle - a community minded youth leader and artist.

📍 **Dr. Sammy Lee Square**

4.6 *W Olympic Blvd & Irolo St, LA 90006* Honors first Asian American to win an Olympic gold medal for the U.S.

📍 **Vermont Square**

3.1 1201 W 48th St, LA 90037.

STATUES

See Memorials, Murals, Museums, Sculpture Gardens, and Watts Towers or go to the Public Art in Public Places or the LA County Arts and Culture webpage and search Civic Arts for more information.

Elgin Baylor Statue
5.9   Chick Hearn Court at Figueroa Blvd and Olympic.

Jackie Robinson Statue:

9.0   *1000 Vin Scully Dr, LA 90012.*

17.7   *1001 Rose Bowl Dr, Pasadena 91103.*

Kareem Abdul Jabbar Statue
5.9   In front of the Staples Center on Chick Hearn Court just off of Figueroa Blvd and Olympic.

Magic Johnson Statue
5.9   Chick Hearn Court just off of Figueroa Blvd and Olympic.

Peace on Earth (1969)
7.8   *N Hope St, LA 90012*
10-ton, 29-foot high bronze sculpture. By Jacques Lipchitz. Music Center Plaza.

STEAK HOUSES

See Restaurants for more food, dining and restaurant-related options.

Fleming's Prime Steakhouse & Wine Bar
5.9   *800 W Olympic Blvd, LA 90015.*

Fogo de Chao Brazilian Steakhouse
800 S Figueroa St, LA 90017.
4.9   All-you-can-eat meat carved tableside plus an extensive salad bar.

Morton's the Steakhouse
5.9   *435 S. La Cienega Blvd., LA 90048.*

Musso and Frank Grill
6667 Hollywood Blvd, Hollywood, 90028.
7.2   Iconic steakhouse, open since 1919 is Hollywood's oldest restaurant.

Sizzler
Casual, sit-down, steak, seafood and salad restaurant.

831 E Manchester Blvd, Inglewood 90301.
4.3

5801 Sepulveda Blvd, Culver City 90230.
4.8

Taylor's Steak House
3361 W 8th St, LA 90005.
4.6   Providing the finest aged, corn-fed prime and certified Angus Beef available at affordable prices.

SWIMMING POOLS

📍 **Athens Park and Swimming Pool**
9.9 *12603 S Broadway, LA 90061.*

📍 **Carson Pool**
17.7 *1001 Rose Bowl Dr, Pasadena 91103.*

📍 **Celes King III Indoor Swimming Pool**
1.2 *5001 Obama Blvd, LA 90016.*

📍 **Central Park and Swimming Pool**
5.4 *1357 E. 22nd St., LA 90011.*

📍 **Edward Vincent Jr. Park and Swimming Pool**
3.4 *700 Warren Ln, Inglewood, 90302.*

📍 **Eleanor Green Roberts Aquatic Center - Indoor Swimming Pool**
2.9 *4526 W Pico Blvd, LA 90019.*

📍 **Green Meadows Swimming Pool**
7.6 *431 E 89th St, LA 90003.*

📍 **Helen Keller Park Swimming Pool**
8.7 *12521 S. Vermont Ave. LA 90044.*

📍 **Hemingway Park Pool**
13.2 *16605 San Pedro St, Carson 90746.*

📍 **Jesse Owens Park Indoor Swimming Pool**
5.7 *9835 S Western Ave, LA 90047.*

📍 **LA84/ John C. Argue Swim Stadium**
3.3 *3980 Bill Robertson Ln, LA 90037.*
Site of 1984 Olympics.

Lennox Park Swimming Pool

6.5 *10828 S. Condon Ave. Inglewood 90304.*

Lynwood Natatorium

14.0 *3770 MLK Jr. Blvd, Lynwood 90262.*
Olympic size facility.

Van Ness Park + Recreation Center + Swimming Pool

2.3 *5720 2nd Ave, LA 90043.*

Weingart YM Wellness & Aquatic Center/Indoor Swimming Pool

7.1 *9900 S Vermont Ave, LA 90044.*

109th Street Pool

13.2 *1500 E 109th St, LA 90059.*

T

TACOS

Millions of taco trucks. Here's two brick and mortar spots. See Restaurants for more options.

📍 **Taco Mell**
0.5 *4326 Crenshaw Blvd, LA 90008.*

📍 **Worldwide Tacos**
2419 W King Blvd, LA 90008.
1.0 Freshly preparing over 150 different Tacos.

TAI CHI

📍 **Dharma Health Institute**
143 Culver Blvd, Playa Del Rey 90293.
9.6 Acupuncture, Qi Gong, Tai Chi, and Yoga.

📍 **Westside Tai Chi**
4095 Overland Ave, Culver City 90232.
4.9 Yang style Tai Chi.

TEA SHOPS

See Cafe's and Coffee for more information.

📍 **LA Grind Coffee & Tea Bar**
3.6 *1412 S Redondo Blvd, LA, 90019.*

📍 **Sip and Sonder**
4.7 *108 S Market Street Inglewood, 90301.*

TENNIS COURTS

Love tennis? Here's a shortlist of open play tennis courts in South LA.

📍 **Algin Sutton Recreation Center**
6.6 *8800 South Hoover St., LA 90044.*

📍 **Darby Park Tennis Courts**
4.6 *3400 W Arbor Vitae St, Inglewood 90305.*

📍 **Dignity Health Sports Park & Tennis Courts**
15.0 *18400 S Avalon, Carson 90746.*
Located on the campus of CSUDH.

📍 **East Rancho Dominguez Park Recreation Center**
17.3 *15116 S. Atlantic Ave. Compton, 90221.*
Best known as the park where venus and Serena Williams learned how to play tennis.

📍 **Edward Vincent Jr. Park Tennis Courts**
3.2 700 Warren Ln, Inglewood 90302.

📍 **Jackie Tatum/Harvard Recreation Center**
3.8 *1535 W 62nd St., LA 90047.*

📍 **Jim Gilliam Park and Recreation Center**
2.9 *4000 S La Brea Ave, LA 90008.*

📍 **Lafayette Multipurpose Community Center**
6.0 *625 S. Lafayette Park Place, LA 90057.*

Loren Miller Recreation Center
3.3   *2717 Halldale Ave., LA 90018.*

Queen Anne Recreation Center
3.0   *1240 West Blvd., LA 90019.*

Ross Snyder Recreation Center
5.3   *1501 East 41st St., LA 90011.*

Saint Andrews Recreation Center
4.8   *8701 St. Andrews Pl., LA 90047.*

Van Ness Recreation Center
2.3   *5720 2nd Ave, LA 90043.*

Venus and Serena Williams Tennis Courts and Academy
1.2   *5001 Obama Blvd. LA, 90016.*
Comprehensive educational tennis program.   Open courts.

THAI TOWN

See Cities and Neighborhoods Around South LA for more information.

THEATERS

See Concert Venues, Movie Theaters, and Performing Arts for more information.

Greek Theater
9.2   *2700 N Vermont Ave, LA 90027.*

John Anson Ford Theater
8.3
2580 Cahuenga Blvd, LA 90068.
Eclectic music, dance, theatre, film and family events.

Orpheum Theater
6.8
842 S Broadway, LA 90014.
Art deco.

Saban Theater
5.5
8440 Wilshire Blvd. Beverly Hills 90211.
Art deco.

The Wiltern Theater
4.4
3790 Wilshire Blvd. LA 90010.
Art Deco performing arts theater.

Vision Theater
0.8
3341 W 43rd Place, LA 90008.

YouTube Theater
4.9
1011 Stadium Dr, Inglewood 90305.

TOURS

Self-guided and docent led tours of South LA. Sign up for the Go Crenshaw website newsletter for more information.

TOWERS

Watts Towers
12.8
1727 E. 107th St. LA 90002.
Built by Simon Rodia. California Historical Landmark #993.

TRAILS

See Hiking, Nature Parks, Preserves, Reserves, Walking Paths, etc for more information.

Marvin Braude Trail
13.3 *15100 Ocean Front Walk, Pacific Palisades, 90272.*

Park to Playa Trailhead
3.1 Thirteen mile trail from Baldwin Hills to the beach.

TRAINS

Angel's Flight Railway
350 S Grand Ave, LA 90071.
6.6 The world's shortest funicular. LA Historic-Cultural Landmark #4.

Griffith Park & Southern Railroad
4400 Crystal Springs Dr, LA 90027.
14.2 Ride one mile course on mini-locomotive..

LA Union Station aka Amtrak Station LAX
800 N Alameda St, LA, 90012.
8.3 Hub of LA's Metro Rail and Bus System, the Metrolink Commuter Train System, and Amtrak.

Travel Town Railroad
5200 Zoo Dr, LA 90027.
17.2 Locomotive museum and mini-train ride.

Watts Train Station
1686 E 103rd St, LA 90002.
10.5 LA Historic-Cultural Landmark #36.

U

UNIVERSITIES

Refer to Colleges for more information.

📍 **California State University, Dominguez Hills**
15.9 *Carson 90747.*

📍 **California State University, Los Angeles**
12.9 *LA 90032.*

📍 **Charles Drew University of Medicine and Science**
1731 E 120th St, LA 90059.
12.1 California's only HBCU (historically black college/university).

📍 **Loyola Marymount University**
8.6 *LA 90045.*

📍 **University of California, Los Angeles**
LA 90095.
10.7 Home of the Bruins.

📍 **University of Southern California**
3.3 *LA 90007.*

V

VEGAN/VEGETARIAN FOOD

See Restaurants for more food, dining and restaurant-related options.

Azla Ethiopian Vegan Cuisine
0.5   *4309 Leimert Blvd, LA 90008.*

Baba's Vegan Cafe
6619 S. Western Ave, LA 90047.
3.6   Pop-Up every last Sunday at Leimert Park Artwalk.

Simply Wholesome Health Food Restaurant and Store
2.6   *4508 W Slauson Ave, LA 90043.*

Swift Vegan Cafe
4279 Crenshaw Blvd, LA 90008.
0.5   Serving Plant-based meals inspired by Indian, Thai, Caribbean and South American cuisines.

VENICE

See Cities and Neighborhoods Around South LA for more info.

VIEW PARK/WINDSOR HILLS

See Cities and Neighborhoods Around South LA for more info.

WALKING GROUPS

There are a lot of walking groups, and places to walk, in South LA. Search the internet for more information.

Crenshaw Walks
0.7
4315 Leimert Blvd, LA 90008.
Offers year-round health and fitness programs in Crenshaw, Baldwin Hills and Leimert Park.

WALKING PATHS

See Arboretums, Art Walks, Beaches, Bike Paths, Botanical Gardens, Caves, Exercise, Lakes, Nature Parks, Parks, Preserves, Reservoirs, Trails, Wetlands, Wildlife, etc,... for more information.

Angels Walk LA — Self-Guided Tours
Go to the Angels Walk LA website for details.

1.6
Angels Walk Crenshaw.

7.8
Angels Walk Figueroa Corridor.

8.5
Angels Walk Union Station.

Augustus Hawkins Nature Park
6.5 *5790 Compton Ave, LA 90011.*

Ballona Wetlands State Ecological Reserve
7.9 *Playa Del Rey 90293.*

Deforest Park Wetlands
19.3 *Long Beach 90805.*
Interpretive signage.

Destination Crenshaw Open-Air Museum (Planned)
1.1 Open-air public art space. Crenshaw Blvd between Vernon and Slauson.

Dockweiler Beach
11.3 *12000 Vista Del Mar, PDR 90293.*

Dominguez Gap Wetlands
21.4 *Long Beach, 90807.*
Urban escape along the LA River with trails for hiking, biking, bird-watching & horseback riding.

Earvin Magic Johnson Park
11.3 *1050 E 120th St, LA 90059.*

Echo Park Lake
8.6 *751 Echo Park Ave, LA 90026.*

Hollywood Reservoir/Lake Hollywood
8.9 *LA 90068.*
Three mile loop. Views of Hollywood Sign.

Hollywood Walk of Fame
7.2 The world's most famous sidewalk. Hollywood and Vine.

Kenneth Hahn State Recreation Area

2.3 *4100 S. La Cienega Blvd, LA 90056.*
Dog friendly, 1.9 mile loop hiking, walking, and trail running with scenic views.

Latino Walk of Fame

12.3 *4726 Whittier Blvd, East LA 90022.*

Marsh Street Nature Park

12.9 *2944 Gleneden St, LA 90039.*

Promenade of Prominence

9.5 *103rd and Success Street, LA 90002.*
Honors locals and national figures.

Rodeo Drive Walk of Style

6.7 *328 N Rodeo Dr, Beverly Hills, CA 90210.*
Honors fashion icons.

Sankofa Passage

0.8 *43rd and Degnan, LA 90008.*
Honors artistic excellence.

Sepulveda Basin Wildlife Reserve

18.3 *6416 Woodley Ave, Van Nuys 91406.*

South Los Angeles Wetlands Park

5.1 *5413 S Avalon Blvd, LA, CA 90011.*

Universal Studios CityWalk

11.1 *100 Universal City Plaza, Universal City 91608.*

Venice Beach Boardwalk

9.3 *1800 Ocean Front Walk, Venice 90291.*

📍 **Watts Towers Crescent Greenway**
10.5   *Watts 90002.*

WATER PARKS

See Aquatic Centers, Beaches, Lakes and Swimming Pools for more information.

📍 **Alondra Park Splash Pad**
12.4   *3850 Manhattan Beach Blvd, Lawndale 90260.*

📍 **Great Wolf Lodge Water Park**
36.3   *12681 Harbor Blvd, Garden Grove 92840.*

📍 **Knott's Soak City**
8039 Beach Blvd, Buena Park 90620.
28.2   Seasonal water park.

WATERMELONS

Watermelons can be found at roadside stands throughout South LA. Here's one.

📍 **Sam's Watermelons**
4.1   *6223 Normandie Ave, LA 90044.*

WATTS

See Cities and Neighborhoods Around South LA for more information.

WESTWOOD

See Cities and Neighborhoods Around South LA for more information.

WETLANDS

See Arboretums, Art Walks, Beaches, Bike Paths, Caves, Exercise, and Hiking Trails, Lakes, Nature Parks and Preserves, Reservoirs, Walking Paths,Wetlands, and Wildlife Reserves, etc,... for more information about walking paths and hiking trails.

Augustus Hawkins Nature Park + Wetlands + Nature Museum
6.4 *5790 Compton Ave., LA 90011.*
Nine acre retreat.

Ballona Wetlands State Ecological Reserve
7.9 *Playa Del Rey 90293.*

Deforest Park Wetlands
19.3 *Long Beach 90805.*
Wildlife habitat, native plants and interpretive signage.

Dominguez Gap Wetlands
21.4 *Long Beach, 90807.*
Urban escape along the LA River with trails for hiking, biking, bird-watching & horseback riding.

South Los Angeles Wetlands Park
5.1 *5413 S Avalon Blvd, LA, CA 90011.*

WILDLIFE REFUGES & SANCTUARY

Seal Beach National Wildlife Refuge
800 Seal Beach Blvd, Seal Beach 90740.
31.0   Encompasses 965 acres.

Sepulveda Basin Wildlife Reserve
6416 Woodley Ave, Van Nuys 91406.
18.3   Lake, birds and butterflies.

Star Eco Station Wildlife Rescue Museum
10101 Jefferson Blvd, Culver City, 90232.
3.7   Birds, reptiles and rescued wildlife.

Tujunga Ponds Wildlife Sanctuary
21.4   *Sunland-Tujunga, 91040.*

WILLOWBROOK

See Cities and Neighborhoods Around South LA for more information.

WINE AND WINERIES

See Bars and Breweries.

Adams Wine Shop & Bar
5359 W Adams Blvd, LA 90016.
3.3   Black-owned wine shop and bar.

Angelino Wine Company
8.6   *1646 N. Spring St, LA 90012.*

Charles Wine Company

11.5   *3235 N. San Fernando Road, Unit 1F, LA 90006.*
Black owned.

Pips on La Brea

3.4   *1356 S. La Brea Ave, LA 90019.*
Restaurant. Bar. Wine. Live Jazz. Italian food.

San Antonio Winery

9.0   *737 Lamar St, LA 90031.*
LA's oldest winery.

The Blending Lab Winery

5.8   *7948 W. 3rd Street, LA 90048.*
Urban winery tasting room.

1010 Wine and Events

3.3   *1010 N La Brea Ave, Inglewood 90302.*
Black-owned wine bar features the largest selection of
black-owned wines in the state of California.

X

MALCOLM X COMMEMORATION SITE

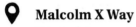

Malcolm X Way

4.6 Central Ave and Martin Luther King. Jr. Blvd.

Y

YOGA

Namaste Y'all!

Crenshaw Dance and Yoga Studio
1.7   *5426 Crenshaw Blvd, LA 90043.*

Dharma Health Institute
9.6   *143 Culver Blvd, Playa Del Rey 90293.*
Acupuncture, Qi Gong, Tai Chi, and Yoga.

Krishna Kaur/10th Gate Yoga
4.1   *1035 S Cloverdale Ave, LA 90019.*
Kundalini Yoga.

Sivananda Yoga Center
2.1   *3741 W 27th St, LA 90018.*
Hatha yoga.

YOGURT

Like "fro-yo"? See Ice Cream for more information.

Menchie's Frozen Yogurt
5.3   *5622 Sawtelle Blvd, Culver City 90230.*

Pinkberry
6000 Sepulveda Blvd, Culver City 90230.
0.1   Inside the mall.

YogurtTalk
0.1   *3650 W Martin Luther King Jr Blvd, LA 90008.*

YogurtLand:

3939 Crenshaw Blvd, LA 90008.
0.1

5375 W Centinela Ave, LA, CA 90045.
4.4

5375 W Centinela Ave, LA, CA 90045.
12.4

Z

ZOOLOGICAL EXHIBITIONS

See Arboretums, Aquariums, Gardens, Petting Zoos, Wetlands and Wildlife for more information.

LA Zoo & Botanical Gardens
13.6
5333 Zoo Dr, LA 90027.
Home to more than 2,200 mammals, birds, amphibians, and reptiles. The botanical garden features over 800 different plant species.

Old LA Zoo
13.4
4801 Griffith Park Dr, LA 90027.
Founded in 1912, this now-abandoned zoo offers past enclosure ruins, picnic space & hiking trails.

FORTY ONE THINGS TO DO ON CRENSHAW BLVD LISTED FROM A TO Z

SPOTLIGHT ON CRENSHAW BLVD

Also known as The Crenshaw District, is a neighborhood in South LA, California. In the post-World War II era a Japanese-American community was established in Crenshaw. Later, African-Americans started migrating to the district in the mid 1960s, and by the early 1970s were the majority. Crenshaw Blvd is the beating heart center of LA's African American community.

Angeles Funeral Home
0.4
3875 Crenshaw Blvd. LA 90008.
Designed by Paul R. Williams. Los Angeles Historic-Cultural Monument #774.

Best Buy Meat Co.
2.5
7108 S. Crenshaw Blvd. LA 90043.
Offering Chicken Sausage, Shrimp Sausage, Turkey Chops, Chicken and other poultry and meat options.

California Cannabis
2.7
7415 Crenshaw Blvd, LA 90043.
Black owned.

Crenshaw Dance and Yoga
1.7
5426 Crenshaw Blvd, LA 90043.

Crenshaw Square
0.4
3870 Crenshaw Blvd, LA 90008.
Dining. Restaurant & Bar. Shopping. Hair. Nails. Shoes. Etc.

Delicious Southern Cuisine
0.7
4371 Crenshaw Blvd, LA 90008.

Destination Crenshaw Open-Air Museum (Planned)
1.1 Open-air public art space. Crenshaw Blvd between Vernon and Slauson.

Dulan's Soul Food Restaurant
1.1 *4859 Crenshaw Blvd, LA 90043.*

Earle's Grill Restaurant
0.5 *3864 Crenshaw Blvd, LA 90008.*

Gilbee's Shoe Repair
0.4 3870 Crenshaw Blvd #104, LA 90008.

Gorilla Rx Wellness
0.3 *4233 S Crenshaw Blvd, LA 90008.*
Black owned cannabis.

Gus's World Famous Fried Chicken
2.8 *1262 Crenshaw Blvd, LA 90019.*
Memphis-borne chain for spicy fried chicken & comfort sides.

Iconic South LA Palm Tree Lined Avenues
0.7 *Obama Blvd between Crenshaw Blvd and La Brea Ave.*

Krispy Kreme Donuts
0.1 *4034 Crenshaw Blvd, LA 90008.*
See 'em made through the glass window. Kids 12 and under get one free donut per visit.

Los Angeles Sentinel/LA Watts Times
0.6 *3800 Crenshaw Blvd, LA 90008.*
African American owned and operated.

Lula Washington Dance Theater
0.5 *3773 Crenshaw Blvd, LA 90016.*

Marilyn's Soul Food
1.5 *2638 Crenshaw Blvd, LA 90016.*

Mayor Tom Bradley Post Office
3894 Crenshaw Blvd. LA 90008.
0.4 Named for LA's first African American Mayor.

Mayor Tom Bradley Square
3894 Crenshaw Blvd., LA 90008.
0.4 Honors the 38th Mayor of Los Angeles.

The Metaphor Club
4333 Crenshaw Blvd, LA 90008.
0.6 Writer's lounge.

Moorimgoong Martial Arts
3.0 *1149 Crenshaw Blvd, LA 90019.*

Museum of African American Art Los Angeles
4005 Crenshaw Blvd, LA 90008.
0.1 On the 3rd floor of Macy's

NE Conaway Peanuts
3818 Crenshaw Blvd, LA 90008.
0.6 South LA's best roasted peanuts.

Nipsey Hussle Mural
LA 90043.
1.7 Near Crenshaw Blvd and Slauson.

Nipsey Hussle Square
Intersection of Crenshaw and Slauson, 90043.
2.2 Honors the vision of Nipsey Hussle—a community minded youth leader and artist.

Orleans and York Deli + Cajun Cafe

2.7 *3868 Crenshaw Blvd LA 90008.*

Phillips Bar-B-Que Take-Out Restaurant

1.6 *2619 Crenshaw Blvd, LA 90016.*
Popular take-out spot.

Right Choice Caribbean Market

0.2 *4233 Crenshaw Blvd, LA 90008.*

Swift Vegan Cafe

0.5 *4279 Crenshaw Blvd, LA 90008.*

Crenshaw Line:

Crenshaw Blvd/Exposition Blvd.
0.9

Crenshaw Blvd/MLK Jr Blvd.
0.0

Crenshaw Blvd/Vernon.
0.9

Tak's Coffee Shop

0.5 *3870 Crenshaw Blvd #101, LA 90008.*
Hawaiian and Asian influenced dishes.

Taco Mell

0.5 *4326 Crenshaw Blvd, LA 90008.*

Taste of Soul Festival

0.0 *On Crenshaw Blvd from Exposition to Vernon.*
Annually in October.

The District Restaurant and Bar
0.3 *3888 Crenshaw Blvd, LA 90008.*

The Elixir Mural
Painted by Patrick Henry Johnson. Located just south
0.3 of the intersection of Crenshaw Blvd and Stocker.

The Great Wall of Crenshaw Mural
Painted by graffiti collective Rocking The Nation.
1.5 Crenshaw Blvd at 50th St.

YogurtLand:
0.1 *3939 Crenshaw Blvd, LA 90008.*

ZamZam Perfumes and Essential Oils
0.1 *4293 Crenshaw Blvd, LA 90008.*

TWENTY-FOUR THINGS TO DO IN CULVER CITY LISTED FROM A TO Z

SPOTLIGHT CULVER CITY

Soaked in movie making history, Culver City features studio tours, a buzzing dining and nightlife scene,globally inspired eateries, gastropubs and cozy cocktail bars.

📍 **ArcLight Movie Theaters Culver City**
4.2 *9500 Culver Blvd, Culver City 90232.*

📍 **Ballona Creek**
Starts in Culver City. Runs 9 miles from Baldwin Hills
3.5 to the Pacific Ocean.

📍 **Ballona Creek Bike Path**
Culver City 90232.
3.5 Enter on Duquesne Ave near Jefferson Blvd.

📍 **Big Lou's Toys & Collectibles and Slot Car Racing Mall**
5.0 *5413 Sepulveda Blvd, Culver City 90230.*
Spacious shop packed with toys & collectibles, plus a slot-car track for racing events.

📍 **Boneyard Dog Park**
3.6 *Duquesne Ave, Culver City 90230.*

📍 **Cliffs of Id**
2537 *S Fairfax Ave, Culver City 90232.*
3.2 Climbing walls.

📍 **Culver City Senior Center**
4.6 *095 Overland Ave, Culver City 90232.*

📍 **Culver City Skate Park**
3.5 *9910 Jefferson Blvd, Culver City 90232.*

Julian Dixon Library
4.7 *4975 Overland Ave, Culver City 90230.*

Lucilles's Smokehouse
5.0 *6000 Sepulveda Blvd, Culver City 90230.*
Inside mall.

Malik Books
4.8 *6000 Sepulveda Blvd, Suite 2470, Culver City 90230.*

Menchie's Frozen Yogurt
5.3 *5622 Sawtelle Blvd, Culver City 90230.*

Mr. Bones Pumpkin Patch
3.7 *10100 Jefferson Blvd., Culver City 90232.*
Brings the farm to the city and celebrates the magic of Halloween.

Pinkberry
0.1 *6000 Sepulveda Blvd, Culver City 90230.*
Inside the mall.

Sizzler Steak House
4.8 *5801 Sepulveda Blvd, Culver City 90230.*

Sony Pictures Studio Tour
4.4 *10202 Washington Blvd, Culver City, 90232.*
A two-hour guided walking tour.

Star Eco Station Wildlife Rescue Museum
3.7 *10101 Jefferson Blvd, Culver City, 90232.*
Birds, reptiles and rescued wildlife.

Stoneview Nature Center and Demonstration Garden

3.0

5950 Stoneview Dr. Culver City, 90232.

Urban sanctuary nestled in the Western Baldwin Hills with scenic views of the Santa Monica.

West LA College

4.9

9000 Overland Ave, Culver City 90230.

Westside Tai Chi

4.9

4095 Overland Ave, Culver City 90232.

Yang style Tai Chi.

What Wall (1998)

3.2

3524 Hayden Ave, Culver City 90232.

By Eric Moss for Culver City's Architecture as Art program.

Woodside Mural (2014)

3.9

8970 Washington Blvd, Culver City 90232.

By Jason Woodside.

THIRTY ONE THINGS PLUS TO DO IN INGLEWOOD LISTED FROM A TO Z

SPOTLIGHT ON INGLEWOOD

Inglewood is a city in southwestern Los Angeles County, California, in the Los Angeles metropolitan area. As of the 2010 U.S. Census, the city had a population of 109,673. It was incorporated on February 14, 1908.

Banadir Somali Restaurant
5.2 *137 Arbor Vitae St, Inglewood 90301.*

Cuban Leaf Cigar Lounge
3.7 *424 E. Florence Ave. Inglewood, 90301.*

Darby Park SkateBoard Area
3400 W Arbor Vitae St, Inglewood 90305.
4.6 Park has playground & areas for picnics, tennis, basketball, skateboards & field sports.

Drobe Stogies
3.2 *1322 N. La Brea Ave, Inglewood, 90302.*

Dulan's Soul Food Restaurants:
4.5 *202 E Manchester Blvd, Inglewood 90301.*

Edward Vincent Jr. Park and Swimming Pool
3.4 *700 Warren Ln, Inglewood, 90302.*

Grevillea Art Park
101 E Kelso St, Inglewood 90301.
4.7 World's largest petrachrome mural.

Halal Kabob House
1117 W Manchester Blvd, Unit G, Inglewood 90301.
5.5 Pakistani.

Hilltop Coffee, Cafe + Kitchen
4.3 *170 N. La Brea Ave, Inglewood, 90301.*

Hollywood Park Casino
5.5 *3883 W Century Blvd, Inglewood, 90303.*
Casino and sports bar.

Inglewood Farmers Market
4.5 *Market St and Manchester Blvd, Inglewood 90301.*

Inglewood Senior Citizens Center
3.8 *330 Centinela Ave, Inglewood 90302.*

Jamz Creamery
4.7 *231 E. Manchester Blvd, Inglewood 90301.*

Kenji's Kajukenbo Academy
3.4 *1212 N. La Brea Ave., Inglewood 90302.*

Kindness, Joy, Love and Happiness (KJLH 102.3 FM)
161 N La Brea Ave, Inglewood, 90301.
Contemporary R&B 24/7. Owned by Stevie Wonder.

La Michoacana Ricas Nieves y Paletas
4.6 *303 W Manchester Blvd, Inglewood 90301.*

Lavender Blue Restaurant & Lounge
3.9 *3310 W. Manchester Blvd, Inglewood, 90305.*
Jazz, blues and food.

Lennox Park Swimming Pool
6.5 *10828 S. Condon Ave. Inglewood 90304.*

Market Street Shopping District
4.5 *100 N. Market St, Inglewood 90301*

Morningside Park Reservoir

4.1   *Inglewood 90305.*

Motherland Music Drums

4.1   *601 N Eucalyptus Ave, Inglewood 90302.*
African drums, supplies, custom drum making, repairs
and maintenance, instruction and performances.

Mr. Fries Man

5.3   *1120 W Florence Ave #C, Inglewood 90301.*
World-famous. Black-owned.

Mutiara Food & Market

3.3   *225 S La Brea Ave, Inglewood 90301.*
Indonesian and Malaysian.

Nothing But the Blues Radio Program
Broadcast Saturdays from 2:00 PM until 6:00 PM, and
Sunday from 2:00 PM until 7:00 PM PST. Hosted by
Gary Wagner on KJZZ radio station 88.1 FM.

Orleans and York Deli + Cajun Cafe:

4.0   *400 E Florence Ave Inglewood 90301.*

Phillips Bar-B-Que Take-Out Restaurant

1.6   *2619 Crenshaw Blvd, LA 90016.*

Randy's Donuts

5.4   *805 West Manchester Blvd, Inglewood, CA 90301.*
Three 3 locations in South LA, only the original location
features the iconic giant donut.

Rosalie's Caribbean Cuisine

4.6   *446 S Market St #2310, Inglewood 90301.*
See also Shabazz Bakery.

Roscoe's House of Chicken and Waffles
5.1 *621 West Manchester Blvd, Inglewood 90301.*

Savoy Entertainment Center
218 South La Brea Ave, Inglewood, 90301.
4.5 Located in DT Inglewood.

Shabazz Bakery
446 S Market St #2310, Inglewood 90301.
4.6 See also Rosalie's Caribbean Cuisine.

Sip and Sonder
4.7 *108 S Market Street Inglewood, 90301.*

Sizzler Steak House
4.3 *831 E Manchester Blvd, Inglewood 90301.*

Sofi Stadium and Entertainment Complex
4.8 *1001 Stadium Dr, Inglewood 90301.*

The Debonair Cigar Lounge
3.9 *1111 S. La Brea Ave, LA 90019.*

The Forum
7.1 *3900 W Manchester Blvd, Inglewood 90305.*

The Wood Bar-B-Que and Sports Lounge
4.2 *129 N Market St, Inglewood 90301.*

Woody's Bar-B-Q
3.5 *475 S. Market St., Inglewood 90301.*

1010 Wine and Events
1010 N La Brea Ave, Inglewood 90302.
3.3 Black-owned.

FIFTEEN THINGS TO DO ON LA BREA LISTED FROM A TO Z

SPOTLIGHT ON LA BREA

📍 **Iconic South LA Palm Tree Lined Avenues**
0.7 *Obama Blvd between Crenshaw Blvd and La Brea Ave.*

📍 **Jim Gilliam Recreation Center**
1.5 *4000 South La Brea Ave, LA 90008.*

📍 **Norman O. Houston Park**
2.3 *4800 S. La Brea, LA 90008.*
Walking path lined with fitness equipment.

📍 **Drobe Stogies**
3.2 *1322 N. La Brea Ave, Inglewood, 90302.*

📍 **Kenji's Kajukenbo Academy**
3.4 *1212 N. La Brea Ave., Inglewood 90302.*

📍 **Pips on La Brea**
3.4 *1356 S. La Brea Ave, LA 90019.*
Restaurant. Bar. Wine. Live Jazz. Italian food.

📍 **The Debonair Cigar Lounge**
3.9 *1111 S. La Brea Ave, LA 90019.*

📍 **Hilltop Coffee, Cafe + Kitchen**
2.4 *170 N. La Brea Ave, Inglewood, 90301.*

📍 **Mutiara Food & Market**
3.3 *225 S La Brea Ave, Inglewood 90301.*
Indonesian and Malaysian.

📍 **Savoy Entertainment Center Nightclub**
4.8 *218 South La Brea Ave, Inglewood 90301.*

La Brea Tar Pits and Museum
5.2 *5801 Wilshire Blvd, LA 90036.*

Pink's Hot Dogs
6.0 *709 N La Brea Ave, LA 90038.*

Bludso's Bar & Que
6.6 *609 N La Brea Ave, LA 90036.*

SIXTY THREE THINGS TO DO IN LEIMERT PARK LISTED FROM A TO Z

SPOTLIGHT ON LEIMERT PARK

Dubbed the "Black Greenwich Village" by filmmaker John Singleton, Leimert Park is the heart of LA's African American cultural community. Leimert Park showcases the best of Black LA. Check out the monthly Leimert Art Walk. Shop for art, fashion and jewelry. Have a cup of coffee. Try the BBQ, spicy Jamaican cuisine, vegan cuisine or tantalizing soul food. LA 90008 and 90043.

📍 **Ackee Bamboo Jamaican Restaurant**
0.5   *4305 Degnan Blvd, LA 90008.*

📍 **African Marketplace, Farmers Market and Drum Circle**
0.5   *43rd and Degnan, LA 90008.*
Sundays 10 am to 5 pm.

📍 **Angeles Funeral Home**
3875 Crenshaw Blvd. LA 90008.
0.4   Designed by Paul R. Williams. Los Angeles Historic-Cultural Monument #774.

📍 **Art + Practice Exhibition Space**
0.7   *3401 W 43rd Pl, LA 90008.*

📍 **Azla Ethiopian Vegan Cuisine**
0.5   *4309 Leimert Blvd, LA 90008.*

📍 **Baldwin Hills Crenshaw Plaza Mall**
0.1   *3650 W. King Blvd, LA 90008.*

📍 **Baldwin Hills Crenshaw Plaza Free Summer Concert Series**
0.3   *3650 W MLK Jr Blvd, LA, 90008.*
Free.

Barbara Morrison Performing Arts Center
0.6   *4305 Degnan Blvd, LA 90008.*

California Cannabis
2.7   *7415 Crenshaw Blvd, LA 90043.*
Black owned.

California Jazz and Blues Museum
0.7   *4317 Degnan Blvd, LA 90008.*

Cinemark Movie Theaters Baldwin Hills Crenshaw
0.2   *4020 Marlton Ave, LA 90008.*

Crenshaw Walks
4315 Leimert Blvd, LA 90008.
0.7   Padded walking path lined by fitness equipment.

Crenshaw YMCA
0.4   *3820 Santa Rosalia Dr, LA 90008.*

Debbie Allen Dance Academy
3.4   *1850 S Manhattan Pl, LA 90019*

Delicious Southern Cuisine
0.7   *4371 Crenshaw Blvd, LA 90008.*

Doris Japanese Garden
La Cienega Blvd, LA 90008.
4.1   In Kenneth Hahn Park.

Dulan's Soul Food Restaurant
1.1   *4859 Crenshaw Blvd, LA 90043.*

Earle's Grill Restaurant
0.5   *3864 Crenshaw Blvd, LA 90008.*

Fernando Pullum Community Arts Center
0.7 *3351 W. 43rd St., LA 90008.*
Youth arts center.

Gorilla Rx Wellness
0.3 *4233 S Crenshaw Blvd, LA 90008.*
Black owned cannabis.

Harun's Coffee + Cafe
0.7 *4336 Degnan Blvd, LA 90008.*

Heavenly Cakes Creations
1.5 *2916 W Vernon Ave, LA 90008.*

Hot and Cool Coffee + Cafe
0.7 *4331 Degnan Blvd, LA 90008.*

KAOS Network
4343 Leimert Blvd, LA 90008.
0.7 Offers artistically talented youth and art enthusiasts
a warm open environment to enjoy trans-media and
multimedia art disciplines.

Krispy Kreme Donuts
4034 Crenshaw Blvd, LA 90008.
0.1 See 'em made through the glass window. Kids 12 and
under get one free donut per visit.

Leimert Park Fountain
0.6 *4395 Leimert Blvd, LA 90008.*

Leimert Park Garden Tour
Annual self-guided tour held in May. Check the
internet for dates.

Leimert Park Jazz Festival
4020 Marlton Ave, LA 90008.
0.2 Annually in August.

Leimert Park Village Plaza
4395 Leimert Blvd., LA 90008.
1.0

Los Angeles Sentinel/LA Watts Times
3800 Crenshaw Blvd, LA 90008.
0.6 African American owned and operated.

Malik Books
0.2 *3650 W. Martin Luther King Blvd. Suite # 245. LA 90008.*

Mayor Tom Bradley Square
3894 Crenshaw Blvd., LA 90008.
0.4 Honors the 38th Mayor of Los Angeles.

The Metaphor Club
4333 Crenshaw Blvd, LA 90008.
0.6 Writer's lounge.

Museum of African American Art Los Angeles
4005 Crenshaw Blvd, LA 90008.
0.1 On the 3rd floor of Macy's.

Nappily Naturals Beauty Apothecary
4342 Degnan Blvd, LA 90008.
0.7 Culturally inspired natural beauty and health store.

NE Conaway Peanuts
3818 Crenshaw Blvd, LA 90008.
0.6 South LA's best roasted peanuts.

Nipsey Hussle Mural
LA 90043.
1.7   Near Crenshaw Blvd and Slauson.

Norman O. Houston Park + Trails
4800 S. La Brea, LA 90008.
2.3   Pathway lined with fitness equipment.

Orleans and York Deli + Cajun Cafe
2.7   *3868 Crenshaw Blvd LA 90008.*

Pan African Film Festival
4020 Marlton Ave, LA 90008.
0.2   Annually in February.

Post and Beam
0.3   *3767 Santa Rosalia Dr, LA 90008.*
Restaurant. Bar. Patio. Frequent live jazz.

Regency West (Leimert Park)
3339 W. 43rd St., LA 90008.
0.6   Banquet Hall and local gathering spot.

Rueben Ingold Park
4400 W Mt Vernon Dr, View Park 90043.
2.0   Surfaced walkway and workout equipment.

Ride On Bike Co-op
4319 Degnan Blvd, LA 90008.
0.6   Full service bicycle shop.

Salsa At The Shaw
3650 W. MLK Jr. Blvd., LA 90008.
0.2   At the Crenshaw Plaza Farmers Market 10 am to 3 pm.
Last Saturday of the month.

Sanchez Ranch Adobe

0.7

#487. 3725 Don Felipe Dr, LA 90008.
Built in 1790. Los Angeles Historic-Cultural Monument

Sankofa Passage Sidewalk

0.8

Begins at 43rd and Degnan, LA 90008.
Honors South LA's artistic excellence.

Sika

0.6

4330 Degnan Blvd, LA 90008.
African style jewelry.

Southern Girl Bakery & Cafe

0.2

3650 W MLK Jr Blvd. LA 90008.

Stocker Corridor Trail

0.7

Stocker St & Presidio Dr, LA 90008.

Swift Vegan Cafe

0.5

4279 Crenshaw Blvd, LA 90008.

Tak's Coffee Shop

0.5

3870 Crenshaw Blvd #101, LA 90008.
Hawaiian and Asian influenced dishes.

The District Restaurant and Bar

0.3

3888 Crenshaw Blvd, LA 90008.

The Last Stand = Unite (2001)

0.7

4331 Degnan Blvd, LA 90008.
By Carla Carr. Located in the alley on the south side of Hot and Cool Cafe.

Thrive Health Lab

1.6

3701 W. 54th St, LA 90043.

Vision Theater - Designated Cultural Arts Center
3341 W 43rd Place, LA 90008.
0.8 Performing arts, music, dance, theater venue.

World Stage Performance Gallery
4344 Degnan Blvd, LA 90008.
0.8 Jazz-oriented educational and performance art space.

Worldwide Tacos
1.0 *2419 W King Blvd, LA 90008.*

YogurtTalk
0.1 *3650 W Martin Luther King Jr Blvd, LA 90008.*

YogurtLand
0.1 *3939 Crenshaw Blvd, LA 90008.*

ZamZam Perfumes and Essential Oils
0.1 *4293 Crenshaw Blvd, LA 90008.*

ELEVEN THINGS TO DO ON PICO BLVD LISTED FROM A TO Z

SPOTLIGHT ON PICO BLVD

Catch One Nightclub (CON)
2.9 *4067 Pico Blvd, LA 90019.*

Eleanor Green Roberts Park
2.9 *4526 W Pico Blvd, LA 90019.*

Gilbert Lindsey Plaza
1201 Figueroa Dr, LA 90015.
5.7 Located on the corner of Figueroa and Pico.

Mateo's Ice Cream & Fruit Bars
4234 W Pico Blvd, LA 90019.
2.4 Paletas y nieve de frutas naturales.

Museum of Tolerance
6.2 *9786 Pico Blvd, LA 90035.*

My Two Cents LA
4.2 *5583 W Pico Blvd, LA 90019.*

Papa Christo's Greek Restaurant, Deli and Taverna
2771 Pico Blvd, LA 90006.
4.5 Market & no-frills restaurant

Pips on La Brea
1356 S. La Brea Ave, LA 90019.
3.4 Restaurant. Bar. Wine. Live Jazz. Italian food.

Rancho Park Golf Course
7.5 *10460 W Pico Blvd, LA, 90064.*

Roscoe's House of Chicken and Waffles

3.5   *5006 Pico Blvd, LA 90019.*

Versailles Cuban Restaurant

4.7   *1415 S La Cienega Blvd, LA 90035.*
Just south of Pico. Offering traditional Cuban dishes.

FIFTEEN THINGS TO DO ON WASHINGTON BLVD LISTED FROM A TO Z

SPOTLIGHT ON WASHINGTON BLVD

Brasil Brasil Cultural Center
7.1   *12453 Washington Blvd, LA 90066.*
Offers classes in Capoeira, Samba, Zumba Hip-Hop, Drumming and Dance.

Capoeira Brasil LA
3.6   *5557 Washington Blvd, LA 90016.*

Ginger's Divine Ice Cream and Pops
7.2   *12550 W Washington Blvd, LA 90066.*

LA Libreria
3.0   *4732 W Washington Blvd, LA 90016.*

Nate Holden Performing Arts Center & Ebony Repertory Theater
2.6   *4708 W Washington Blvd, LA 90016.*

Natraliart Jamaican Restaurant
2.7   *3426 W. Washington Blvd, LA 90018.*

Ray Charles Memorial Library
3.6   *2107 W Washington Blvd, LA 90018.*

Reparations Club
2.8   *4636 W. Washington Blvd. LA. 90016.*

Simply D'Licious
2.5   *4641 W Washington Blvd, LA 90016.*

Sony Pictures Studio Tour
4.4   *10202 Washington Blvd, Culver City, 90232.*
A two-hour guided walking tour.

Soriana Halal Restaurant

5.4 *512 E Washington Blvd, LA 90015.*
Arabian.

Tut's Egyptian Cuisine

7.2 *12114 W Washington Blvd, LA 90066.*

Washington Irving Branch Library

2.3 *4117 W Washington Blvd, LA 90018.*

Wellington Square Farmers Market

2.5 *4394 W Washington Blvd, LA 90016.*

Woodside Mural (2014)

3.9 *8970 Washington Blvd, Culver City 90232.*
By Jason Woodside.

ELEVEN THINGS TO DO ON WEST ADAMS BLVD LISTED FROM A TO Z

SPOTLIGHT ON WEST ADAMS

Adams Wine Shop & Bar
3.3 *5359 W Adams Blvd, LA 90016.*
Black-owned wine shop and bar.

Alta Adams "Soul Food"
2.6 *5359 W Adams Blvd, LA 90016.*

Delicious Vinyl Pizza Restaurant
2.8 *5419 W Adams Blvd, LA 90016.*

Fais Do Do Cafe Nightclub
2.3 *5257 W Adams Blvd, LA 90016.*

Honey Bee's House of Breakfast
1.8 *4715 W Adams Blvd, LA 90016.*

Johnny's Pastrami
1.6 *4327 W Adams Blvd, LA 90007.*

LA84/ John C. Argue Swim Stadium
3.3 *3980 Bill Robertson Ln, LA 90037.*
Site of 1984 Olympics.

Mizlala West Adams
5400 West Adams Blvd, LA 90016.
2.6 Local neighborhood mediterranean grill.

Peace Awareness Labyrinth and Gardens
2.0 *3500 W Adams Blvd, LA 90018.*

Taqueria Los Anaya - Mexican Restaurant
4651 W Adams Blvd, LA 90016.
3.0 Taqueria Los Anaya specializes in authentic Mexican
food, made with love and care.

The Cork Bar and Grill

1.9 *4771 W. Adams Blvd, LA 90016.*

Vee's Cafe

1.3 *5418 W Adams Blvd, LA 90016.*

GO SOUTH LA: A TO Z BY DISTANCE FROM MLK JR BLVD AND CRENSHAW BLVD

ZONE ONE: 0 MILES TO 5.0 MILES FROM KING X CRENSHAW

📍 **Taste of Soul Festival**
0.0   *On Crenshaw Blvd from Exposition to Vernon.*
Annually in October.

📍 **Baldwin Hills Crenshaw Plaza Mall**
0.1   *3650 W. King Blvd, LA 90008.*

📍 **Black Santa**
0.1   Baldwin Hills Crenshaw Mall

📍 **Museum of African American Art Los Angeles**
0.1   *4005 Crenshaw Blvd, LA 90008.*
On the 3rd floor of Macy's

📍 **Krispy Kreme Donuts**
0.1   *4034 Crenshaw Blvd, LA 90008.*
See 'em made through the glass window. Kids 12 and under get one free donut per visit.

📍 **YogurtLand**
0.1   *3939 Crenshaw Blvd, LA 90008.*

📍 **YogurtTalk**
0.1   *3650 W Martin Luther King Jr Blvd, LA 90008.*

📍 **ZamZam Perfumes and Essential Oils**
0.1   *4293 Crenshaw Blvd, LA 90008.*

📍 **Cinemark Movie Theaters Baldwin Hills Crenshaw**
0.2   *4020 Marlton Ave, LA 90008.*

📍 **Crenshaw Farmers Market**
0.2 Located on the grounds of the BHCP mall.
Saturday 10 am to 3 pm.

📍 **Malik Books:**
0.2 *3650 W. Martin Luther King Blvd. Suite # 245. LA 90008.*

📍 **Pan African Film Festival**
4020 Marlton Ave, LA 90008.
0.2 Annually in February.

📍 **Right Choice Caribbean Market**
0.2 *4233 Crenshaw Blvd, LA 90008.*

📍 **Salsa At The Shaw**
3650 W. MLK Jr. Blvd., LA 90008.
0.2 At the Crenshaw Plaza Farmers Market 10 am to 3 pm.
Last Saturday of the month.

📍 **Southern Girl Bakery & Cafe**
0.2 *3650 W MLK Jr Blvd. LA 90008.*

📍 **Baldwin Hills Crenshaw Plaza Free Summer Concert Series**
0.3 *3650 W MLK Jr Blvd, LA, 90008.*
Free.

📍 **Hotville Chicken**
0.3 *4070 Marlton Ave. LA 90008.*

📍 **Post and Beam**
3767 Santa Rosalia Dr, LA 90008.
0.3 Restaurant. Bar. Patio. Frequent live jazz.

📍 **The District Restaurant and Bar**
0.3 *3888 Crenshaw Blvd, LA 90008.*

The Elixir Mural
0.3
Painted by Patrick Henry Johnson. Located just south of the intersection of Crenshaw Blvd and Stocker.

African American Cultural Center
0.4
3018 W 48th St, LA 90043.
Promotes knowledge and appreciation of African American culture.

Angeles Funeral Home
0.4
3875 Crenshaw Blvd, LA 90008.
Home to many famous end-of-life "going-home" celebrations including Johnny Cochran and Barry White.

Baldwin Hills Crenshaw
0.4
A South Los Angeles neighborhood.

Crenshaw YMCA
0.4
3820 Santa Rosalia Dr, LA 90008.

Gilbee's Shoe Repair
0.4
3870 Crenshaw Blvd #104, LA 90008.

Leimert Park Art Walk
0.4
43rd and Degnan.
Last Sunday of the Month. 2pm to 8pm.

Mayor Tom Bradley Post Office
0.4
3894 Crenshaw Blvd. LA 90008.
LA's first African American and longest serving Mayor.

Mayor Tom Bradley Square
0.4
3894 Crenshaw Blvd., LA 90008.
Honors the 38th Mayor of Los Angeles.

Ackee Bamboo Jamaican Cuisine & Adassa's Cafe - Restaurant

0.5   *4305 Degnan Blvd, LA 90008.*

African Marketplace

43rd and Degnan, LA 90008.

0.5   Sundays 10 am to 5 pm.

Azla Ethiopian Vegan Cuisine

0.5   *4309 Leimert Blvd, LA 90008.*

Earle's Grill Restaurant

3864 Crenshaw Blvd, LA 90008.

0.5   All of the hot dogs are gourmet and cooked individually with care and to perfection on an open flame grill, while still maintaining the juicy and satisfying flavors of the dog.

Leimert Park Village Book Fair

0.5   Annual event held in August.

Los Angeles Sentinel/LA Watts Times

3800 Crenshaw Blvd, LA 90008.

0.6   African American owned and operated.

Lula Washington Dance Theater

0.5   *3773 Crenshaw Blvd, LA 90016.*

Swift Vegan Cafe

0.5   *4279 Crenshaw Blvd, LA 90008.*

Taco Mell

0.5   *4326 Crenshaw Blvd, LA 90008.*

Tak's Coffee Shop
3870 Crenshaw Blvd #101, LA 90008.
0.5   Hawaiian and Asian influenced dishes.

Barbara Morrison Performing Arts Center
0.6   *4305 Degnan Blvd, LA 90008.*

Leimert Park Fountain
0.6   *4395 Leimert Blvd, LA 90008.*

Los Angeles Sentinel/LA Watts Times
3800 Crenshaw Blvd, LA 90008.
0.6   African American owned and operated.

NE Conaway Peanuts
3818 Crenshaw Blvd, LA 90008.
0.6   South LA's best roasted peanuts.

Regency West (Leimert Park)
3339 W. 43rd St., LA 90008.
0.6   Banquet Hall and local gathering spot.

Ride On Bike Co-op
4319 Degnan Blvd, LA 90008.
0.6   Full service bicycle shop.

Sika
4330 Degnan Blvd, LA 90008.
0.6   African style jewelry.

The Metaphor Club
4333 Crenshaw Blvd, LA 90008.
0.6   Writer's lounge.

Art + Practice Exhibition Space
0.7   *3401 W 43rd Pl, LA 90008.*

California Jazz and Blues Museum

0.7   *4317 Degnan Blvd, LA 90008.*

The Last Stand = Unite (2001)

4331 Degnan Blvd, LA 90008.

0.7   By Carla Carr. Located in the alley on the south side of Hot and Cool Cafe.

Delicious Southern Cuisine

0.7   *4371 Crenshaw Blvd, LA 90008.*

Fernando Pullum Community Arts Center

3351 W. 43rd St., LA 90008.

0.7   Youth arts center.

Hot and Cool Coffee + Cafe

0.7   *4331 Degnan Blvd, LA 90008.*

Sanchez Ranch Adobe

#487. 3725 Don Felipe Dr, LA 90008.

0.7   Built in 1790. Los Angeles Historic-Cultural Monument

Stocker Corridor Trail

0.7   *Stocker St & Presidio Dr, LA 90008.*

KAOS Network

0.7   *4343 Leimert Blvd, LA 90008.*

Harun's Coffee + Cafe

0.7   *4336 Degnan Blvd, LA 90008.*

Nappily Naturals Beauty Apothecary

4342 Degnan Blvd, LA 90008.

0.7   Culturally inspired natural beauty and health store.

📍 **Neighbors Skate Shop**
0.7 *4344 Degnan Blvd, LA 90008.*

📍 **Heart of Hyde Park**
5726 Crenshaw, LA 90043.
0.8 By Moses Ball and LA Commons

📍 **Juneteenth Celebration**
43rd and Degnan.
0.8 Annually in June.

📍 **President Barack Obama Blvd**
0.8 *Runs between La Cienega Blvd and Western Ave.*

📍 **Samba in the Streets**
4343 Leimert Blvd, LA, CA 90008.
0.8 Go to "Viver Brasil" website for information.

📍 **Sankofa Passage Sidewalk**
Begins at 43rd and Degnan, LA 90008.
0.8 Honors South LA's artistic excellence.

📍 **Vision Theater - Designated Cultural Arts Center**
3341 W 43rd Place, LA 90008.
0.8 Performing arts, music, dance, theater venue.

📍 **World Stage Performance Gallery**
0.8 *4344 Degnan Blvd, LA 90008.*

📍 **Leimert Park Village Plaza**
1.0 *4395 Leimert Blvd., LA 90008.*

📍 **Walk a Mile in My Shoes Civil Rights Memorial**
1.0 Located at the corner of King and Obama.

Worldwide Tacos

1.0 *2419 W King Blvd, LA 90008.*

Destination Crenshaw Open-Air Museum (Planned)

1.1 Open-air public art space. Crenshaw Blvd between Vernon and Slauson.

Dulan's Soul Food Restaurant

1.1 *4859 Crenshaw Blvd, LA 90043.*

Celes King III Indoor Swimming Pool

1.2 *5001 Obama Blvd, LA 90016.*

Charmette Bonpua Skate Plaza Park

1.2 *5001 Rodeo Rd, LA 90016.*

Heavenly Cakes Creations

1.5 *2916 W Vernon Ave, LA 90008.*

Marilyn's Soul Food

1.5 *2638 Crenshaw Blvd, LA 90016.*

View Park-Windsor Hills

1.5 The unincorporated View Park-Windsor Hills neighborhood is on the north end of South LA along Angeles Vista Boulevard and the Windsor Hills neighborhood is on the southern end to the north of Slauson Avenue.

Women Do Get Weary But They Don't Give Up (1990)

1.5 *3720 West 54th, LA 90043.*
By Alice Patrick.

Angeles Mesa Library

1.6 *2700 W 52nd St, LA 90043.*

📍 **Angels Walk Crenshaw**
1.6   Go to the Angels Walk LA website for details.

📍 **Johnny's Pastrami**
1.6   *4327 W Adams Blvd, LA 90007.*

📍 **Phillips Bar-B-Que Take-Out Restaurant**
      2619 Crenshaw Blvd, LA 90016.
1.6   Popular take-out spot.

📍 **Thrive Health Lab**
1.6   *3701 W. 54th St, LA 90043.*

📍 **Crenshaw Dance and Yoga Studio**
      5426 Crenshaw Blvd, LA 90043.
1.7   Offers all levels of Yoga and dance classes.

📍 **Dr. Martin Luther King Jr Park**
1.7   *3916 South Western Ave., LA 90062.*

📍 **Lopez Flowers**
1.7   *3409 S. La Brea Blvd. LA 90016.*

📍 **Love is For Everyone (1990)**
      5149 West Jefferson Blvd, LA 90016.
1.7   By Mary Linn-Hughes and Reginald Zachary. Located on Sycamore Street on the west side of the Minority AIDS Project Building.

📍 **Nipsey Hussle Mural**
      LA 90043.
1.7   Near Crenshaw Blvd and Slauson.

📍 **Archbishop Carl Bean Square**
1.8   *Corner of W. Jefferson Blvd. and S. Sycamore Ave, 90016.*
Dedicated to the founder of the Minority AIDS Project
and the Unity Fellowship Church Movement.

📍 **Honey Bee's House of Breakfast**
1.8   *4715 W Adams Blvd, LA 90016.*

📍 **Sweet E's Bake Shop**
1.8   *4574 W Adams Blvd, LA 90016.*

📍 **Visions and Motions (1992)**
1.8   *4828 Crenshaw Blvd, LA 90043.*
By Elliot Pickney. On the side of the Community Youth
Sports & Arts Foundation.

📍 **Black Seed (1990)**
1.9   *2301 W. Jefferson Blvd, LA 90018.*
By Eddie Orr, David Mosley and William T. Stubbs.

📍 **Mary McLeod Bethune Regional Library**
1.9   *3900 S Western Ave, LA 90062.*

📍 **View Park Bebe Moore Campbell Library**
1.9   *3854 W 54th St, LA 90043.*

📍 **The Cork Bar and Grill**
1.9   *4771 W. Adams Blvd, LA 90016.*

📍 **Walk a Mile in My Shoes Civil Rights Memorial**
1.9   Located at Jefferson and Obama Blvd.

📍 **Baldwin Hills Library**
2.0   *2906 South La Brea Ave, LA 90016.*

Rueben Ingold Park + Walking Course
2.0
4400 W Mt Vernon Dr, View Park 90043.
Surfaced walkway and workout equipment.

Peace Awareness Labyrinth and Gardens
2.0
3500 W Adams Blvd, LA 90018.

Jefferson Library
2.1
2211 W Jefferson Blvd, LA 90018.

Normandie French Bakery & Bistro
2.6
3022 S Cochran Ave, LA 90016.

Sivananda Yoga Vedanta Center LA
3741 W 27th St, LA 90018.
2.1
Traditional yoga for health and peace of mind.

Troubled Island (2003)
2520 W View Street, LA 90016.
2.1
By Artist Noni Olabisi.

William Grant Still Arts Center - Designated Cultural Arts Center
2.1
2520 S W View St, LA 90016.
Offers camps, workshops, music/art classes for adults youth, exhibitions, concerts, and community meetings.

Hilltop Coffee, Cafe + Kitchen
2.4
4427 W Slauson Ave, LA 90043.

Nipsey Hussle Square
Intersection of Crenshaw and Slauson, 90043.
2.2
Honors the vision of Nipsey Hussle—a community minded youth leader and artist.

Primo's Bike Shop
2.2 *1645 W Vernon Ave, LA 90062.*

Fais Do Do Cafe
2.3 *5257 W Adams Blvd, LA 90016.*

Norman O. Houston Park + Trails
4800 S. La Brea, LA 90008.
2.3 Pathway lined with fitness equipment.

Kenneth Hahn State Recreation Area Hiking + Walking Loop
2.3 *4100 S. La Cienega Blvd, LA 90056.*
 Two miles loop. Dog friendly. Scenic views.

Van Ness Park + Recreation Center + Swimming Pool
2.3 *5720 2nd Ave, LA 90043.*

Washington Irving Branch Library
2.3 *4117 W Washington Blvd, LA 90018.*

Kenneth Hahn State Park Disc Golf Course
2.4 *4100 S La Cienega Blvd, LA 90056.*

Mateo's Ice Cream & Fruit Bars
4234 W Pico Blvd, LA 90019.
2.4 Paletas y nieve de frutas naturales.

New Orleans Snoballs
4452 W Slauson Ave, Windsor Hills 90043.
2.4 Shaved ice.

Best Buy Meat Co.
2.5
7108 S. Crenshaw Blvd. LA 90043.
Offering Chicken Sausage, Shrimp Sausage, Turkey Chops, Chicken and other poultry and meat options.

Pepper's Jamaican Belizean Cuisine
2.5
2166 W Slauson Ave, LA 90047.

Quebobs Mediterranean Restaurant
2.5
3560 S La Cienega Blvd, Unit F, LA 90016.

Simply D'Licious
2.5
4641 W Washington Blvd, LA 90016.

Wellington Square Farmers Market
2.5
4394 W Washington Blvd, LA 90016.

Ahmanson Senior Citizen Center
2.6
3990 Bill Robertson Ln, LA 90037.

Alta Adams "Soul Food"
2.6
5359 W Adams Blvd, LA 90016.
An inclusive setting, serving comforting food and great cocktails that bring people together in community.

See's Candy Factory
2.6
3431 S La Cienega Blvd, LA 90016.

Simply Wholesome Health Food Restaurant + Store
2.6
4508 W Slauson Ave, LA 90043.
Tasty, nutritious food and health products.

Jerusalem Chicken
2.6
4448 W Slauson, LA 90043.
A Palestinian Chicken Eatery.

La Louisianne Cajun Creole Soul Food Restaurant
2.6   *5812 Overhill Dr, LA 90043.*

Mizlala West Adams
2.6   *5400 West Adams Blvd, LA 90016.*

Nate Holden Performing Arts Center & Ebony Repertory Theater
2.6   *4708 W Washington Blvd, LA 90016.*
Designated Cultural and World-class performing arts center.

Roy A. Anderson Recreation Center
2.6   *3980 Bill Robertson Lane, LA 90037.*

Freedom Won't Wait (1992)
1815 W 54th St., LA 90062.
2.7   By Artist Noni Olabisi.

Ladera Park Recreation Center
2.7   *6027 Ladera Park Ave, LA 90056.*

Lucas Museum of Narrative Art (Planned)
2.7   *Exposition Park, LA 90007.*

Natraliart Jamaican Restaurant
2.7   *3426 W. Washington Blvd, LA 90018.*

Orleans and York Deli + Cajun Cafe:
2.7   *3868 Crenshaw Blvd LA 90008.*

Delicious Vinyl Pizza Restaurant
2.8   *5419 W Adams Blvd, LA 90016.*

Gus's World Famous Fried Chicken
2.8   *1262 Crenshaw Blvd, LA 90019.*

📍 **Reparations Club**
2.8 *3054 S Victoria Ave, LA 90016*

📍 **Catch One Nightclub (CON)**
2.9 *4067 Pico Blvd, LA 90019.*

📍 **Jim Gilliam Park and Recreation Center**
2.9 *4000 S La Brea Ave, LA 90008.*

📍 **LA84 Foundation Sport History Library**
2.9 *2141 W Adams Blvd, LA 90018.*

📍 **LA Memorial Coliseum**
2.9 *3911 S Figueroa St, LA, 90037.*
Home to the 1932, 1984 and 2022 Olympic Games.

📍 **Baldwin Hills Scenic Overlook Hiking + Walking Trail**
3.0 *6300 Hetzler Rd, Culver City 90232.*
Hilltop park with views of Downtown Los Angeles plus hiking trails & history exhibits.

📍 **Banc of California Stadium in Exposition Park**
3.0 *3939 S. Figueroa Ave, LA 90037.*
Home of the LA Football Club.

📍 **Brother Bar-B-Que**
3.0 *7725 Crenshaw Blvd, LA 90043.*

📍 **California African American Museum**
3.0 *600 State Dr. LA 90037.*

📍 **California Science Center Museum**
3.0 *700 Exposition Park Dr. LA 90037.*

Culver City Stairs

3.0 *6105 Hetzler Rd, Culver City, CA 90232*

LA Libreria

3.0 *4732 W Washington Blvd, LA 90016.*
Children's literature in Spanish imported from Latin America & Spain.

Mikes Deli Sandwich Shop Restaurant

3.0 *4859 W. Slauson Ave., LA 90056.*

Moorimgoong Martial Arts

3.0 *1149 Crenshaw Blvd, LA 90019.*

Natural History Museum of LA County

3.0 *900 W Exposition Blvd, LA 90007.*

Stoneview Nature Center and Demonstration Garden

3.0 *5950 Stoneview Dr. Culver City, 90232.*

Space Shuttle Endeavor - Rocket/Space Ship Museum

3.0 *700 Exposition Park Dr, LA 90037.*

Taqueria Los Anaya

3.0 *4651 W Adams Blvd, LA 90016.*
Taqueria Los Anaya specializes in authentic Mexican food, made with love and care.

Yvonne B. Burke Senior Community Center

3.0 *4750 W 62nd St, LA 90056.*

Park to Playa Hiking + Walking Trailhead

3.1   A 13-mile regional trail connecting the Baldwin Hills Parklands to the Pacific Ocean.

Queen Anne Recreation Center

3.1   *1240 West Blvd, LA 90019.*

Queen of Sheba Ethiopian Restaurant

3.1   *630 N. La Brea #106, Inglewood 90302.*

Vermont Square

3.1   *1201 W 48th St, LA 90037.*

Centinela Springs Marker

3.2   *700 Warren Ln, Inglewood, 90302.*
California Historical Landmark #363

Cliffs of Id

3.2   *2537 S Fairfax Ave, Culver City 90232.*
Climbing walls.

Drobe Stogies

3.2   *1322 N. La Brea Ave, Inglewood, 90302.*

Edward Vincent Jr. Park

3.2   *700 Warren Ln, Inglewood, 90302.*

Kenneth Hahn State Recreation Area

3.2   *4100 S. La Cienega Blvd, LA 90056.*

Loren Miller Recreation Center

3.2   *2717 S Halldale Ave, LA 90018.*

What Wall (1998)
3524 Hayden Ave, Culver City 90232.
3.2   By Eric Moss for Culver City's Architecture as Art program.

Halal Food
1905 S Western Ave, LA 90018.
3.3   Indian.

Historic Palm Tree of Los Angeles
500 Exposition Park Dr, LA 90037.
3.3   Read the marker describing the oldest palm tree in the city.

John C. Argue Swim Stadium
3.3   *3980 Bill Robertson Ln, LA 90037.*

Loren Miller Recreation Center
3.2   *2717 S Halldale Ave, LA 90018.*

University of Southern California
LA 90007.
3.3   Home of the Trojans.

Debbie Allen Dance Academy
3.4   *1850 S Manhattan Pl, LA 90019.*

Kang Nam - Traditional Korean Restaurant
4103 W Olympic Blvd, LA, 90019.
3.4   Traditional Korean & Japanese cuisine, from stews to sushi, served in a polished space with a patio.

Kenji's Kajukenbo Academy
3.4   *1212 N. La Brea Ave., Inglewood 90302.*

LA Judo Club
3.4   *3923 W Olympic Blvd, LA 90019.*

Pips on La Brea
3.4
1356 S. La Brea Ave, LA 90019.
Restaurant. Bar. Wine. Live Jazz. Italian food.

Vermont Square Branch Library
3.4
1201 W 48th St, LA 90037.
The oldest branch library in the Los Angeles City Public Library system.

Ballona Creek Bike Path
3.5
Culver City 90232.
Accessible from the Crenshaw District by going west on Jefferson Blvd until you reach Duquesne Ave. Enter on Duquesne Ave near Jefferson Blvd.

Ballona Creek Walking Trail
3.5
Walking, Biking, Running and Walking trail that runs to the ocean and back.

Culver City Skate Park
3.5
9910 Jefferson Blvd, Culver City 90232.

Dave's Hot Chicken
3.5
5301 W Centinela Ave, LA 90045.

IMAX Movie Theater California Science Center
3.5
700 Exposition Park Dr, LA 90037.

Roscoe's House of Chicken and Waffles
3.5
5006 Pico Blvd, LA 90019.

Woody's Bar-B-Q
3.5
475 S. Market St., Inglewood 90301.

Baba's Vegan Cafe
3.6
6619 S. Western Ave, LA 90047.

Country Style Jamaican Cuisine

3.6 *4305 Degnan Blvd, LA 90008.*

Boneyard Dog Park

3.6 *Duquesne Ave, Culver City 90230.*

California Science Center Kelp Forest

3.6 *700 Exposition Park Dr, LA 90037.*

Exposition Park Rose Garden

3.6 *701 State Dr, LA 90037.*
Seven acre garden.

Karuba's Yardy Kitchen

3.6 *4305 Degnan Blvd, LA 90008.*

Ray Charles Memorial Library

3.6 *2107 W Washington Blvd, LA 90018.*

Barbeque King

3.7 *5309 Vermont Ave, LA 90037.*

Cuban Leaf Cigar Lounge

3.7 *424 E. Florence Ave. Inglewood, 90301.*

Mr. Bones Pumpkin Patch

3.7 *10100 Jefferson Blvd., Culver City 90232.*

Star Eco Station - Environmental + Rescued Wildlife Museum

3.7 *10101 Jefferson Blvd, Culver City, 90232.*
Tours, summer camps and exhibits. Over 200+ birds, reptiles & other rescued wildlife.

📍 **Inglewood Senior Citizens Center**

3.8 *330 Centinela Ave, Inglewood 90302.*

📍 **Jackie Tatum/Harvard Recreation Center**

3.8 *1535 W 62nd St., LA 90047.*

📍 **Queen Park Learning Garden**

3.8 *652 E. Queen St, Inglewood 90301.*

📍 **Dr. Martin Luther King Jr Civil Rights Memorial Tree Grove and Commemorative Obelisk**

3.9 Dedicated to MLK Jr. The 15,000 sq. foot tree grove features an obelisk that evokes memories of the 1963 March on Washington for Jobs and Freedom.

📍 **Hyde Park Miriam Matthews Library**

3.9 7150-7156 Arlington Ave, LA 90043.

📍 **Lavender Blue Restaurant Lounge**

3.9 *3310 W. Manchester Blvd., Inglewood, 90305.*
Live jazz and blues with delicious food.

📍 **Mercado la Paloma**

3.9 *3655 S Grand Ave, LA 90007.*

📍 **Newport-Inglewood Fault Zone**

3.9 Forty seven mile long fault starts in Culver City and runs through Inglewood and Newport Beach towards the Pacific Ocean.

📍 **The Debonair Cigar Lounge**

3.9 *1111 S. La Brea Ave, LA 90019.*
See also Shabazz Bakery.

Woodside Mural (2014)
3.9 *8970 Washington Blvd, Culver City 90232.*
By Jason Woodside.

Antioch University
4.0 *400 Corporate Pointe, Culver City, CA 90230.*

Linares Bike Shop
4.0 *4418 S Broadway, LA 90037.*

Shrine Auditorium
665 W. Jefferson Blvd. LA 90007.
4.0 Los Angeles Historic-Cultural Monument #139.

Orleans and York Deli + Cajun Cafe
4.0 *4454 W Slauson Ave, Windsor Hills 90043.*

Doris Japanese Garden
La Cienega Blvd, LA 90008.
4.1 In Kenneth Hahn Park.

El Cholo Mexican Restaurant
4.1 *1121 S Western Ave, LA 90006.*

Kindness, Joy, Love and Happiness (KJLH 102.3 FM)
4.1 *Contemporary R&B 24/7161 N La Brea Ave, Inglewood 90301.*
Owned by Stevie Wonder.

Korean Cultural Center
4.1 *5505 Wilshire Blvd, LA, 90036*

Krishna Kaur/10th Gate Yoga
1035 S Cloverdale Ave, LA 90019.
4.1 Kundalini Yoga as taught by Yogi Bhajan.

📍 **Morningside Park Reservoir**
4.1 *Inglewood 90305.*

📍 **Motherland Music Drums**
4.1 *601 N Eucalyptus Ave, Inglewood 90302.*
African drums and supplies, custom drum making, repairs and maintenance, instruction and performances.

📍 **Phillips Bar-B-Que Take-Out Restaurant**
4.1 *Centinela Ave, Inglewood 90302.*

📍 **Sam's Watermelons**
4.1 *6223 Normandie Ave, LA 90044.*

📍 **ArcLight Movie Theaters Culver City**
4.2 *9500 Culver Blvd, Culver City 90232.*

📍 **Hilltop Coffee, Cafe + Kitchen**
4.2 *170 N. La Brea Ave, Inglewood, 90301.*

📍 **M'Dears Bakery & Bistro**
4.2 *7717 S Western Ave, LA 90047.*
Soul food and desserts.

📍 **The Wood Bar-B-Que and Sports Lounge**
4.2 129 N Market St, Inglewood 90301.

📍 **Sizzler Steak House:**
4.3 *831 E Manchester Blvd, Inglewood 90301.*

📍 **Lavender Blue Restaurant Lounge**
4.4 *3310 W. Manchester Blvd. Inglewood, 90305.*

📍 **Little Belize**
4.4 *17 E. Nutwood St, Inglewood 90301.*

Sony Pictures Studio Tour
4.4 *10202 Washington Blvd, Culver City, 90232.*
A two-hour guided walking tour.

The New Townhouse
4.4 *6835 La Tijera Blvd, LA 90045.*

Wiltern Theater
4.4 *3790 Wilshire Blvd. LA 90010.*
Art Deco style.

YogurtLand:
4.4 *5375 W Centinela Ave, LA, CA 90045.*

Blessed Tropical Cuisine
4.5 *4233 Crenshaw Blvd, LA 90008.*

Dulan's Soul Food Restaurant
4.5 *202 E Manchester Blvd, Inglewood 90301.*

Fox Hills Mall
4.5 *6000 Sepulveda Blvd, Culver City 90230.*

Iman Hasan Square
4.5 *Corner of Central Ave and MLK Jr Blvd.*

Jeang Yuk Jeom Korean BB
4.5 *621 S Western Ave #100, LA 90005.*

Miracle Mile District
4.5 An LA neighborhood that runs along a stretch of Wilshire Boulevard known as Museum Row.

Papa Christo's Greek Restaurant, Deli and Taverna
4.5 *2771 Pico Blvd, LA 90006.*

Southern California Library of South LA
6120 S Vermont Ave, LA 90044.
4.5 Holds extensive collections of histories of community resistance in LA and beyond.

Versailles Cuban Restaurant
4.5 *10319 Venice Blvd, LA 90034.*

Woody's Bar-B-Q
4.5 *1958 W. Florence Ave, LA 90047.*

Culver City Senior Center
4.6 *095 Overland Ave, Culver City 90232.*

Darby Park Skate Board Area
3400 W Arbor Vitae St, Inglewood 90305.
4.6 Park has playground & areas for picnics, tennis, basketball, skateboards & field sports.

Dr. Sammy Lee Square
W Olympic Blvd & Irolo St, LA 90006
4.6 Honors first Asian American to win an Olympic gold medal for the U.S.

La Michoacana Ricas Nieves y Paletas
4.6 *303 W Manchester Blvd, Inglewood 90301.*

Rosalie's Caribbean Cuisine
446 S Market St #2310, Inglewood 90301.
4.6 See also Shabazz Bakery.

Shabazz Bakery
446 S Market St #2310, Inglewood, 90301.
4.6 See Rosalie's Caribbean Cuisine.

Malcolm X Way
4.6 *Central Ave and MLK Jr. Blvd.*

Taylor's Steak House
4.6 *3361 W 8th St, LA 90005.*

Taylor's Steak House
4.6 *3361 W 8th St, LA 90005.*

Grevillea Art Park
4.7 *101 E Kelso St, Inglewood 90301.*
World's largest petrachrome mural.

Jamz Creamery
4.7 *231 E. Manchester Blvd, Inglewood 90301.*

Jayis Ice Cream, Raspados and Popsicles
4.7 *1100 W Florence Ave, LA 90044.*

Julian Dixon Library
4.7 *4975 Overland Ave, Culver City 90230.*

Koreatown Pavilion & Garden
4.7 *1000 Normandie Ave, LA, 90006.*

Lee's Caribbean
4.7 *4233 Crenshaw Blvd, LA 90008.*

Pinkberry
4.7 *6000 Sepulveda Blvd, Culver City 90230.*
Inside the mall.

The History of Transportation (1942)
4.7 *101 E Kelso St, Inglewood 90301.*
By Helen Lundeberg. The largest petrachrome mural in the world

Versailles Cuban Restaurant

4.7 *1415 S La Cienega Blvd, LA 90035.*

Malik Books:

4.8 *6000 Sepulveda Blvd, Suite 2470, Culver City 90230.*

Saint Andrews Recreation Center

4.8 *8701 St. Andrews Pl., LA 90047.*

Savoy Entertainment Center

218 South La Brea Ave, Inglewood, 90301.

4.5 Located in DT Inglewood, the premier choice for LA's urban trendsetters.

Sizzler Steak House:

4.8 *5801 Sepulveda Blvd, Culver City 90230.*

South Park Recreation Center (aka Barry White Park)

4.8 *345 E. 51st St, LA 90011.*

Capoeira Brasil LA

4.9 *5557 Washington Blvd, LA 90016.*

Central Avenue Jazz Festival

4222 S Central Ave, LA 90011.

4.9 Annually in July.

Delicious Southern Cuisine

4229 S. Central Ave, LA 90011.

4.9 At The Historic Dunbar Hotel.

Dunbar Hotel

4225 S Central Ave, LA 90011.

4.9 Former focal point of LA's Black community. Los Angeles Historic-Cultural Monument #131.

📍 **Fogo de Chao Brazilian Steakhouse**
4.9   *800 S Figueroa St, LA 90017.*

📍 **Gilbert Lindsay Skate Park**
4.9   *429 E. 42nd Place, LA 90011.*

📍 **Ground Zero, 1992 LA Rebellion**
4.9   The intersection of Florence and Normandie is considered "ground zero" of the 1992 South LA Rebellion.

📍 **Mount Saint Mary's University Los Angeles**
4.9   *10 Chester Pl, LA 90007.*

📍 **The Little Ethiopia Cultural and Resource Center**
4.9   *1037 S Fairfax Ave, LA, 90019.*

📍 **West LA College**
      9000 Overland Ave, Culver City 90230.
4.9   A two-year, public community college in western Baldwin Hills.

📍 **Westside Tai Chi**
      4095 Overland Ave, Culver City 90232.
4.9   Yang style Tai Chi.

📍 **YouTube Theater**
4.9   *1011 Stadium Dr, Inglewood 90305.*

📍 **Big Lou's Toys & Collectibles and Slot Car Racing Mall**
5.0   *5413 Sepulveda Blvd, Culver City 90230.*
      Spacious shop packed with toys & collectibles, plus a slot-car track for racing events.

Lucilles's Smokehouse

5.0

6000 Sepulveda Blvd, Culver City 90230.
Inside mall.

Our Weekly LA Newspaper

5.0

8732 S Western Ave, LA 90047.
Provides coverage relevant to African-American readers.

ZONE TWO (RED PINS): 5.1 TO 10.0 MILES FROM KING X CRENSHAW

MagIQ Escape Room
5.1 *1446 S Robertson Blvd. LA 90035.*

Roscoe's House of Chicken and Waffles
5.1 *621 W. Manchester Blvd, Inglewood 90301.*

Iman Hasan Square
5.1 *Corner of Central Ave and MLK Jr Blvd.*

South Los Angeles Wetlands Park
5.1 *5413 S Avalon Blvd, LA, CA 90011.*

B. Gerald Cantor Sculpture Garden
5.2 *5905 Wilshire Blvd. LA 90036.*

Banadir Somali Restaurant
5.2 *137 Arbor Vitae St, Inglewood 90301.*

La Brea Tar Pits and Museum
5.2 *5801 Wilshire Blvd, LA 90036.*

Sugar Shack
5.2 *1843 W Imperial Hwy, LA, CA 90047.*
Casual outdoor comedy venue.

Menchie's Frozen Yogurt
5.3 *5622 Sawtelle Blvd, Culver City 90230.*

Ross Snyder Recreation Center
5.3 *1501 East 41st St., LA 90011.*

📍 **Three Weavers Brewing Company**
5.3 *1031 W. Manchester Blvd A-B, Inglewood, CA 90301.*

📍 **Central Park and Swimming Pool**
5.4 *1357 E. 22nd St., LA 90011.*

📍 **Cinemark Movie Theaters at the Promenade**
5.4 *6081 Center Dr, LA 90045.*

📍 **Randy's Donuts**
5.4 *805 West Manchester Blvd, Inglewood, CA 90301.*
Three 3 locations in South LA, only the original location features the iconic giant donut.

📍 **Soriana Halal Restaurant**
5.4 *512 E Washington Blvd, LA 90015.*
Arabian.

📍 **Centinela Adobe Museum**
5.8 *7634 Midfield Ave, LA 90045.*

📍 **Dinah's Diner**
5.5 *6521 S. Sepulveda Blvd, LA 90045.*

📍 **Halal Kabob House**
5.5 *1117 W Manchester Blvd, Unit G, Inglewood 90301.*
Pakistani.

📍 **Hollywood Park Casino**
5.5 *3883 W Century Blvd, Inglewood, 90303.*
Casino and sports bar.

📍 **LA County Museum of Art**
5.5 *5905 Wilshire Blvd, LA, 90036.*

LA County Museum of Art - Jazz at LACMA Series

5.5 *5905 Wilshire Blvd, LA, 90036.*

LA County Museum of Art - LACMA Latin Sounds Music Series

5.5 *5905 Wilshire Blvd, LA 90036.*
Generally runs late May through the end of August.

Paramount Pictures Studio Tour Hollywood

5.5 *5515 Melrose Ave, LA 90038.*

Saban Theater

8440 Wilshire Blvd. Beverly Hills 90211.
5.5 Art deco.

Urban Light

5905 Wilshire Blvd, LA 90036.
5.5 By Chris Burden. Located at LACMA.

El Coyote Mexican Cafe

5.6 *7312 Beverly Blvd, LA 90036.*

The Grove

189 The Grove Dr, LA 90036.
5.6 Very cool mall, next to the historical farmers market, a popular fashion and lifestyle destination offering a mix of retail, restaurants and entertainment.

28th Street YMCA

2800-2812 Paloma St, LA 90011.
5.6 Designed by Paul R. Williams. LA Historic-Cultural Landmark #851.

Gilbert Lindsey Plaza

1201 Figueroa Dr, LA 90015.
5.7 Located on the corner of Figueroa and Pico.

📍 **Granny's Kitchen Southern Style Soul Food**
5.7 *5440 S Central Ave, LA 90011.*

📍 **Jesse Owens Park Indoor Swimming Pool**
5.7 *9835 S Western Ave, LA 90047.*

📍 **The Lexington Bar**
129 E 3rd St, LA 90013.
5.7 Live music and comedy venue with a creative vibe in
the heart of downtown LA.

📍 **Centinela Adobe Museum**
5.8 *7634 Midfield Ave, LA 90045.*

📍 **So-Fi Stadium and Entertainment District at Hollywood Park**
5.8 *3883 W Century Blvd, Inglewood 90303.*
Home of the LA Rams and the LA Chargers.

📍 **Los Angeles Farmers Market**
5.8 *6333 W 3rd St, LA 90036.*

📍 **Shatto 39 Lanes**
3255 W 4th St, LA 90020.
5.8 Basic bowling alley featuring arcade games, several
pool tables & a bar with beer, wine & cocktails.

📍 **The Blending Lab Winery**
7948 W. 3rd Street, LA 90048.
5.8 Urban winery tasting room.

📍 **Elgin Baylor Statue**
5.9 Chick Hearn Court at Figueroa Blvd and Olympic.

📍 **Fleming's Prime Steakhouse & Wine Bar**
5.9 *800 W Olympic Blvd, LA 90015.*

Kareem Abdul Jabbar Statue

5.9

In front of the Staples Center on Chick Hearn Court just off of Figueroa Blvd and Olympic.

Lincoln Theater Historic Site

5.9

2300 S Central Ave, LA 90011.
Hosted shows by Black entertainers during the segregation era. LA Historic-Cultural Landmark #744.

Magic Johnson Statue

5.9

Chick Hearn Court just off of Figueroa Blvd and Olympic.

Morton's the Steakhouse

5.9

435 S. La Cienega Blvd., LA 90048.

Wanda Coleman Library

5.9

120 W Florence Ave, LA 90003.

Franklin D. Roosevelt Park Recreation Center

6.0

7600 Graham Ave, LA 90001.

Maggie Hathaway Golf Course

6.0

1921 W 98th St, LA 90047.
A 9 hole par 3 course located within Jesse Owens Park.

Kobe Bryant Mural (2020)

6.0

1336 Lebanon St, LA 90015.
Search Kobe Bryant murals to find more.

Lafayette Multipurpose Community Center

6.0

625 S. Lafayette Park Place, LA 90057.

Minaco Ventures African Food Market

6.0

8606 ½ S Vermont Ave, LA 90044.
African food, goods and clothes.

Pink's Hot Dogs - Famous Take-Out Hot Dog Stand (Hollywood)

6.0

709 N La Brea Ave, LA 90038.

Creatively topped dogs (some named for celebrities) draw long lines at this historic roadside spot.

Ted Watkins Memorial Park

6.0 *1335 E. 103rd St, LA 90002.*

Los Angeles Trade–Technical College

6.1 *400 W Washington Blvd, LA 90015.*

McArthur Park Lake

9.1 *653 S Alvarado St, LA 90057.*

Regal 15 Cinemas Movie Theater - LA LIVE

6.1 *1000 W Olympic Blvd, LA 90015.*

Staples Center

6.1 *1111 S Figueroa St, LA 90015.*

Music, sports and entertainment center, right in the heart of LA.

El Floridita Restaurant and Nightclub

6.2 *1253 Vine St, LA, CA 90038.*

Live salsa music, dinner and dancing.

Museum of Tolerance

6.2 *9786 Pico Blvd, LA 90035.*

Beverly Center Shopping Mall

6.3 *8500 Beverly Blvd, LA 90048.*

Ginger's Divine Ice Cream and Pops

7.2 *12550 W Washington Blvd, LA 90066.*

Grammy Museum

6.3 *800 W Olympic Blvd, LA 90015.*

Locus City Imprints

11500 S Figueroa St, LA 90061.

6.3 By Steve Appleton. Blue Line Harbor Freeway Station.

Lucky Strike LA Bowling

6.3 *800 W Olympic Blvd, LA 90015.*

Shaquille's Southern Cuisine'

800 W Olympic Blvd, LA 90015.

6.3 Upscale casual restaurant specializing in Southern cuisine. Farm fresh produce and fried chicken.

The Hummus Factory

6.3 *6081 Center Dr, Unit 218, LA 90045.*

Lennox Library

6.4 *4359 Lennox Blvd, Lennox, 90304.*

Levitt Pavilion - 50 Free Summer Concerts

2230 W 6th St, LA, CA 90057.

6.4 Outdoor performance space in McArthur Park, hosting free summer concerts by emerging & name artists.

Santee Alley Shopping

6.4 *210 E Olympic Blvd, LA 90015.*

Sweet Chick's Fried Chicken

448 N Fairfax Ave, LA 90036.

6.4 Fried chicken and waffles.

Westchester Golf Course

7.1 *6900 W Manchester Ave, LA 90045.*

📍 **Augustus Hawkins Nature Park + Wetlands**
6.5 *5790 Compton Ave., LA 90011.*

📍 **Hawthorne Municipal Airport (HHR)**
6.5 *12101 Crenshaw Blvd, Hawthorne 90250.*
General aviation aircraft. Flight training schools.

📍 **OG Cannabis Cafe**
6.5 *1201 N La Brea, West Hollywood 90038.*
Serving farm fresh food, coffee, juice and cannabis daily. Sit on the patio, order a meal, have a conversation and experience cannabis.

📍 **The Mayan Theater and Night Club**
6.5 *1038 S Hill St, LA 90015.*
Formerly a landmark movie palace, currently a nightclub and music venue.

📍 **Algin Sutton Recreation Center**
6.6 *8800 South Hoover St., LA 90044.*

📍 **Angel's Flight Railway**
6.6 *350 S Grand Ave, LA 90071.*
The world's shortest funicular. LA Historic-Cultural Landmark #4.

📍 **Bludso's Bar & Que**
6.6 *609 N La Brea Ave, LA 90036.*

📍 **Los Angeles International Airport (LAX)**
6.6 *One World Way, LA, 90045.*
World's fifth-busiest airport.

📍 **El Cholo Mexican Restaurant**
6.7 *1037 S. Flower St. LA 90015.*

Rodeo Drive Walk of Style

328 N Rodeo Dr, Beverly Hills, CA 90210.

6.7 Honors fashion icons.

West Athens Victory Garden

6.7 *1344 W 105th St, LA, 90044.*

ArcLight Movie Theaters Hollywood

6.8 *6360 Sunset Blvd, LA 90028.*

Hummus House

12211 Hawthorne Blvd, Hawthorne 90250.

6.8 Mediterranean.

Korean BBQ

123 Onizuka St #302, LA 90012.

6.8 In Weller Court.

LA Fashion District

Off 11 St between Los Angeles Street and San Pedro

6.8 Street.

Los Angeles Chinese Cultural Center

1110 Bates Ave, LA, 90029.

6.8 The Los Angeles Chinese Cultural Center (LACCC) was founded in 2005 in the Hollywood area to enrich the community by providing various Chinese cultural programs for all ages.

Orpheum Theater

842 S Broadway, LA 90014.

6.8 Art deco.

Aviation Park

7.0 *11022 Aviation Blvd, LA 90045.*
Sixteen life-size fighter planes Children's playground.
At The Proud Bird Food Bazaar.

Glen Alla Dog Park

7.0 *4601 Alla Rd. Marina Del Rey 90292.*

LA City Hall

7.0 *200 N Spring St, LA 90012.*

Maggie Hathaway Golf Course

1921 W 98th St, LA 90047.
6.0 A 9 hole par 3 course located within Jesse Owens Park.

Proud Bird Food Bazaar and Event Center

7.0 *11022 Aviation Blvd, LA 90045.*
Views of LAX planes, interactive aviation exhibits and
kid-friendly airplane park

Restaurant Row Beverly Hills

7.0 *La Cienega Blvd between Wilshire and San Vicente.*

Brasil Brasil Cultural Center

12453 Washington Blvd, LA 90066.
7.1 Offers classes in Capoeira, Samba, Zumba Hip-Hop,
Drumming and Dance.

Cole's French Dip Restaurant and Bar

7.1 *118 E. 6th St, LA 90014.*

DTLA Salsa Festival

532 S. Olive St., LA 90013.
7.1 Annual July event. Sponsored by the LA Department of
Cultural Affairs. Held in Pershing Square.

The Forum

7.1   *3900 W Manchester Blvd, Inglewood 90305.*

Frances Howard Goldwyn - Hollywood Regional Library

7.1   *1623 Ivar Ave, LA, CA 90028.*

Lucky Strike LA Bowling

7.1   *6801 Hollywood Blvd, Hollywood, 90028.*

Weingart YM Wellness & Aquatic Center/Indoor Swimming Pool

7.1   *9900 S Vermont Ave, LA 90044.*

Westchester Golf Course

7.1   *6900 W Manchester Ave, LA 90045.*

Black Hollywood Education and Resource Center

7.2   *1875 Century Park East, Suite 6th floor, LA 90067.*

Central Public Library DTLA

7.2   *630 W 5th St, LA, 90071.*

El Capitan Theatre

7.2   *6838 Hollywood Blvd, LA 90028.*

Ginger's Divine Ice Cream and Pops

7.2   *12550 W Washington Blvd, LA 90066.*

Hollywood Walk of Fame

7.2   The world's most famous sidewalk. Hollywood and Vine.

Los Angeles City College

7.2   *855 N Vermont Ave, LA 90029.*

📍 **Los Angeles Southwest College**
7.2 *1600 W Imperial Hwy, LA 90047.*

📍 **Musso and Frank Grill**
7.2 *6667 Hollywood Blvd, Hollywood, 90028.*
Iconic steakhouse, open since 1919 is Hollywood's oldest restaurant.

📍 **Otis College of Art and Design**
7.2 *9045 Lincoln Blvd, LA 90045.*

📍 **The Egyptian Movie Theatre**
7.2 *6712 Hollywood Blvd. Hollywood, 90028.*

📍 **The Spare Room**
7.2 7000 Hollywood Blvd, LA 90028.
Cocktail lounge & game parlor. Inside Hollywood Roosevelt Hotel.

📍 **Tut's Egyptian Cuisine**
7.2 *12114 W Washington Blvd, LA 90066.*

📍 **Chinese Theater**
7.3 *6925 Hollywood Blvd, Hollywood 90028.*

📍 **Grand Performances Summer Concert Series**
7.3 *350 S Grand Ave. , LA, 90071.*

📍 **Woodcrest Library**
7.3 *1340 W 106th St, LA, 90044.*

📍 **XLanes LA**
7.3 *333 Alameda St, LA 90013.*

📍 **Eucalyptus Skate Park**
7.4 *12100 S. Inglewood Ave. Hawthorne 90250.*

📍 **Little Tokyo Historic District**

7.4 Heart of the largest Japanese-American population in North America.

📍 **Rodeo Drive**

7.4 Expensive world-famous shopping and dining. Between Wilshire Blvd and Santa Monica Blvd.

📍 **Spring Street Smokehouse Bar-B-Que**

7.4 *640 N. Spring Street, LA 90012.*

📍 **African American Firefighter Museum**

7.6 *1401 S Central Ave, LA 90021.*

📍 **Bryan Hawkins Kenpo Karate**

7.5 *12243 Venice Blvd, LA 90066.*

📍 **Downtown LA Art Walk**

7.5 *W 4th St, LA 90013.*
Galleries, local murals and street art.

📍 **Grand Central Market (DTLA)**

7.5 *317 S Broadway, LA 90013.*
A DTLA landmark since 1917.

📍 **Rancho Park Golf Course**

7.5 *10460 W Pico Blvd, LA, 90064.*

📍 **Viver Brasil Dance Company**

7.5 *2141 N Gower St., LA 90068.*

📍 **African American Firefighter Museum**

7.6 *1401 S Central Ave, LA 90021.*

Beverly Hills

7.6 Home to celebrities, luxury hotels, a restaurant row and Rodeo Drive. The Beverly Hills Gardens Park features fountains and a rose garden. Population 33,709 (2020).

Chester Washington Golf Course

7.6 *1818 Charlie Sifford Dr, LA 90047.*

Green Meadows Swimming Pool

7.6 *431 E 89th St, LA 90003.*

Theme Building at LAX

201 World Way, LA 90045.

7.6 Designed by Paul R. Williams. LA Historic-Cultural Landmark #570.

Westchester Senior Center

7.6 *8740 Lincoln Blvd, LA 90045.*

Avila Adobe Firehouse Museum

7.7 *501 N. Los Angeles St, LA 90012.*

El Pueblo de Los Angeles Historical Monument + Museums

7.7 *125 Paseo De La Plaza, LA, 90012.*

Hong Kong BBQ Restaurant

7.7 *803 N Broadway, LA 90012.*

Japanese American National Museum

7.7 *100 N Central Ave, LA 90012.*

La Placita (The Little Plaza)

125 Paseo De La Plaza, LA 90012.

7.7 Celebrate's LA's birthplace.

Olvera Street

7.7 LA's first street and home of the oldest standing residence in LA's.

Ray's Halal Texas BBQ

7.7 *6038 Santa Fe Ave, Huntington Park 90225.*

Yamashiro's Restaurant Hollywood (Japanese + Chinese)

7.7 *1999 N Sycamore Ave, LA 90068.*
Great restaurant, amazing food, beautifully appointed ground with a fantastic view of LA.

Angels Walk Figueroa Corridor

7.8 Go to the Angels Walk LA website for details.

Hawthorne (see also Airports)

7.8 Incorporated in 1922, the city currently has a population of nearly 87,000.

India's Tandoori Halal Restaurant

7.8 *12866 Hawthorne Blvd, Hawthorne 90250.*
Indian and Pakistani.

Island Reggae Kitchen

7.8 *14426 Crenshaw Blvd, Gardena 90249.*

Peace on Earth (1969)

7.8 *N Hope St, LA 90012*
10-ton, 29-foot high bronze sculpture. By Jacques Lipchitz. Music Center Plaza.

Venice Arts Center for Photography & Film Education

7.8 *13445 Beach Ave, Marina Del Rey 90292.*

📍 **Ballona Wetlands State Ecological Reserve**
7.9 *Playa Del Rey 90293.*

📍 **Bowlero LA**
7.9 *8731 Lincoln Blvd, Westchester 90045.*

📍 **Skid Row**
8.0 A DTLA neighborhood.

📍 **Biddy Mason Memorial Park**
333 S Spring St, LA 90013.
8.1
Featured in the park is *Biddy Mason Time and Place,* an 80-foot-long poured concrete wall by artist Sheila Levrant de Bretteville displaying a timeline of Biddy Mason's life and her freedom papers.

📍 **Chinese American Museum**
8.1 *425 N LA St, LA 90012.*v

📍 **Hollywood Sculpture Garden**
8.1 *2430 Vasanta Way, LA 90068.*

📍 **Japanese Garden**
244 San Pedro St, LA 90012.
8.4
Inside the Japanese American Cultural Center.

📍 **Barnsdall Art Park**
4800 Hollywood Blvd, LA 90027.
8.2
Art classes, museum, tours, theatre and festivals celebrating cultural diversity.

📍 **Japanese Village Plaza**
335 E. 2nd Street, LA 90012.
8.2
Gateway to Little Tokyo.

📍 **Shogun Santa**
8.2 Japanese Village in Little Tokyo.

📍 **Cielito Lindo Restaurant**
8.3 *East 23 Olvera St, LA 90012.*
Since 1934, CL has been serving taquitos, tamales & burritos on historic Olvera Street - the oldest street in LA. Google it to learn more.

📍 **El Paseo Inn Historic Landmark, Restaurant, Bar and Marketplace**
8.3 *11 Olvera St, LA 90012.*
Features mural by artist Rubén Lara Campos.

📍 **John Anson Ford Theater**
8.3 *2580 Cahuenga Blvd, LA 90068.*
Eclectic music, dance, theatre, film and family events.

📍 **Hollywood Bowl**
8.3 *2301 N Highland Ave, LA 90068.*

📍 **Inosanto Academy of Martial Arts**
8.3 *13352 Beach Ave, Marina Del Rey 90292.*

📍 **LA Union Station aka Amtrak Station LAX**
8.3 *800 N Alameda St, LA, 90012.*
Hub of LA's Metro Rail and Bus System, the Metrolink Commuter Train System, and Amtrak.

📍 **Burton Chace Park Summer Concert Series.**
8.4 *13650 Mindanao Way, Marina Del Rey.*

Japanese American Cultural Center
8.4
244 San Pedro St, LA 90012.
A hub for Japanese and Japanese American arts and culture and a community gathering place for the diverse voices it inspires.

The Little Jewel of New Orleans Grocery & Deli Restaurant
8.4
207 Ord St, LA 90012.
Southern-styled market and delicatessen draws its influence from the City of New Orleans.

City of Dreams / River of History
8.5
811 N. Vignes St, LA 90012.
By Richard Wyatt.

Lloyd Taber-Marina del Rey Library
8.5
4533 Admiralty Way, Marina del Rey 90292.

Philippe's Restaurant - The Original French Dip
8.5
1001 North Alameda, LA 90012.

Angelino Wine Company
8.6
1646 N. Spring St, LA 90012.

Echo Park Lake
8.6
751 Echo Park Ave, LA 90026.

Loyola Marymount University
8.6
LA 90045.

Marina Del Rey Harbor
8.6
13755 Fiji Way, MDR 90292.
North America's largest man-made small-craft harbor.

Dub Club - Reggae Night

8.7

1154 Glendale Blvd, LA 90026.

Weekly Wednesday night's at the Echoplex.

Helen Keller Park

8.7

12521 S. Vermont Ave. LA 90044.

Bronson Caves aka The Bat Cave

8.8

3200 Canyon Drive, LA 90068.

Featured in the 1970's TV version of Batman, this 0.6 mile heavily trafficked out and back trail features a cave and is good for all skill levels. Dog-friendly.

Chinatown

8.8

Festive location. Lot's of places to eat and shop. See art galleries, the Taoist Temple, East Gate and the Golden Pagoda. Make a wish at the Seven Star Cavern Wishing Well. Population: 16,557 (2020).

Chinatown Central Plaza

8.9

943 N Broadway, LA 90012.

See the East Gate, Golden Pagoda, and make a wish at the Seven Star Cavern Wishing Well.

Hollywood Reservoir

8.9

LA 90068.

Three mile path. Views of Hollywood Sign.

Two Bit Circus

8.9

634 Mateo St, LA 90021.

Tech-infused Big Top. Interactive entertainment. Free entry. All ages welcome.

Alondra Golf Course

9.0

16400 Prairie Ave. Lawndale, 90260.
This course has two 18 hole courses including a par 3, 18 hole short course.

Hummus Republic

9.0

709 N La Brea Ave, LA 90038.
Mediterranean.

Jackie Robinson Statue

9.0 *1000 Vin Scully Dr, LA 90012.*

Los Angeles River

9.0

The 51-mile river flows through Compton and Long Beach.

Mother's Beach

9.0

4135 Admiralty Way, Marina Del Rey 90292.
Playground. Picnic tables. Kid-friendly. Surf-free sheltered beach.

San Antonio Winery

9.0

737 Lamar St, LA 90031.
LA's oldest winery.

UCLA Marina Aquatic Center

9.1 *14001 Fiji Way, Marina del Rey 90292.*

Greek Theater

9.2 *2700 N Vermont Ave, LA 90027.*

Lakes at El Segundo Golf Course

9.3

400 S Sepulveda Blvd, El Segundo 90245.
Municipal 9-hole golf course offering a driving range, lessons & a cafe.

Venice

9.3

Funky little beach community where gentrification has gone wild. Check out the boardwalk, pier and canal district. Venice 90292.

Venice Beach Boardwalk

9.3

1800 Ocean Front Walk, Venice 90291.

Dodger Stadium

9.4

1000 Vin Scully Ave, LA 90012.

Oakwood Park Recreation Center

9.4

767 California Ave, Venice, 90291.

Venice Beach Recreation Center

9.4

1800 Ocean Front Walk, Venice 90291.

Promenade of Prominence

9.5

103rd and Success Street, LA 90002.
Honors locals and national figures.

Capoeira Besouro

9.6

709 Lincoln Blvd, Venice 90291.

Dharma Health Institute

9.6

143 Culver Blvd, Playa Del Rey 90293.
Acupuncture, Qi Gong, Tai Chi, and Yoga.

Penmar Golf Course

9.6

1233 Rose Ave, Venice, 90291.

Abbot Kinney Memorial Branch Library

9.6

501 Venice Blvd, Venice, 90291.

Chavez Ravine Arboretum

7.9

929 Academy Rd, LA 90012.

The Resurrection of Watts (2001)
10950 South Central Ave, LA 90059.
9.7   By Ras Ammar Nsoroma.

Watts Senior Citizens Center
9.8   *1657 E Century Blvd, LA 90002.*

Westwood Village
Walkable historic district with movie theater,
9.8   restaurants and shops. Home of UCLA.

Athens Park and Swimming Pool
9.9   *12603 S Broadway, LA 90061.*

Santa Monica Airport (SMO)
3233 Donald Douglas Loop, Santa Monica 90405.
9.9   General aviation. Scheduled to close in 2028.

Westminster Dog Park
9.9   *1234 Pacific Avenue Venice 90291.*

Chavez Ridge Disc Golf Course
10.0   *Solano Canyon Dr & Park Row Drive, LA 90012.*

Franklin D Murphy Sculpture Garden
10.0   *245 Charles E Young Dr E, LA, CA 90095.*

Marina Del Rey
10.0   Population: 20,065 (2020).

Mar Vista Branch Library
10.0   *12006 CA-187, LA 90066.*

Pacific Ocean

10.0

22 miles of Pacific Ocean coastline. Numerous beach cities and hundreds of things to do including counting grains of sand.

Venice Beach

10.0

1800 Ocean Front Walk, Venice 90291.

World famous Boardwalk, Muscle Beach and Pier.

ZONE THREE (ORANGE PINS): 10.1 MILES TO 15 MILES

📍 **Griffith Scientific Observatory Museum**
10.1   *2800 E Observatory Rd, LA 90027.*
Look at stars, visit the Samuel Oschin Planetarium, explore the exhibits, and enjoy scenic views of LA.

📍 **LA River Center & Gardens**
10.1   *570 W Ave 26 #100, LA 90065.*
A hidden jewel, sequestered behind thick, ivy covered walls. A wide, circular brick driveway with a spreading ficus tree in the center marks the entrance, and through the arched, wrought-iron gate you get your first glimpse of the fountains, flowers and serenity inside.

📍 **Samuel Oschin Planetarium**
10.1   *2800 E Observatory Rd, LA 90027.*
Visitors can look through a telescope, see a live show iexplore the exhibits, and enjoy the spectacular views of LA and the Hollywood Sign.

📍 **Venice Art Walk**
10.1   Held in May. Features tours, music, food and art.

📍 **Venice Skate Park**
10.1   *800 Ocean Front Walk, Venice 90291.*
Oceanfront skatepark featuring a sunken pool & a street-inspired area with stairs, ledges & rails.

📍 **Santa Monica**
10.2   Coastal city overlooking the Pacific Ocean.

Cecil (1998/1999)
10.3
1727 East 107th Street, Watts 90002.
By Richard Wyatt.

Lighthouse Beach
10.3
4200 Ocean Front Walk, Marina Del Rey, 90292.

Briar Summit Open Space Preserve
10.4
LA 90046.

El Segundo
10.4
This small beachside city serves as the headquarters for many of LA's professional sports teams and is home to the aerospace industry, gastropubs, breweries and the beach.. Hometown on the TV show Sanford and Son. Population: 16,575.

Young People of Watts
10.4
10712 Wilmington Ave., Watts.
By Christena Cardenas.

A. C. Bilbrew Library
10.5
150 E. El Segundo Blvd, LA 90061.

Watts Train Station
10.5
1686 E 103rd St, LA 90002.
LA Historic-Cultural Landmark #36.

Watts Towers Arts Center — Designated Cultural Center
10.5
1727 E. 107th St. LA 90002.

Watts Towers Crescent Greenway
10.5
Watts 90002.

African American Black Resource Center

10.7 *150 E. El Segundo Blvd, LA 90061.*

Looff Hippodrome Carousel

10.7 *1624 Ocean Front Walk, Santa Monica 90401.*
On the Pier.

University of California, Los Angeles

10.7 *LA 90095.*
Home of the Bruins.

UCLA Mildred E. Mathias Botanical Garden

10.8 *707 Tiverton Dr, LA 90095.*

Earvin Magic Johnson Park Lake

10.9 *905 E El Segundo Blvd, LA 90059.*

Victoria Golf Course

11.0 *340 MLK Jr. St. Carson, 90746.*
An LA County Parks and Recreation facility.

Larry Flynt's Lucky Lady Casino

11.1 *1045 Rosecrans Ave, Gardena 90247.*

Silver Lake Reservoir

11.1 *LA 90039.*

Universal Studios CityWalk

11.1 *100 Universal City Plaza, Universal City 91608.*

109th Street Pool

13.2 *1500 E 109th St, LA 90059.*

Dockweiler Beach

11.3 *12000 Vista Del Mar, PDR 90293.*

Universal Studios Hollywood

11.3 100 Universal City Plaza, Universal City 91608.
Film oriented theme park. Rides, dining, shopping, entertainment and seasonal events.

Willowbrook

11.3 Home to MLK Jr. Medical Center, Augustus Hawkins Mental Health Center, Charles Drew University, King/ Drew High School, LA Metro Train Station and the Willowbrook Library.

Willowbrook Library

11.3 *11737 Wilmington Ave, LA 90059.*

Endless Miles

11.4 *12021 Wilmington Ave, LA 90059.*
By Rob Ley. At MLK Jr Medical Campus.

Tongva Park

11.4 *1615 Ocean Ave, Santa Monica, 90401.*
Ocean views.

Cayton's Children Museum

11.5 *395 Santa Monica Place, Santa Monica, 90401.*

Compton Creek Bike Path

11.5 *Compton 90220.*
Runs along the LA River from Compton to Carson.

Drew League Basketball

11.5 *1601 E. 120th St. LA 90059.*
Ballers, street legends and pro's.

Heal the Bay Aquarium

11.5 *1600 Ocean Front Walk, Santa Monica 90401.*

Manhattan Beach

11.5 Home to Bruce's Beach, the site of one of the only Black owned beach resorts in the 1920's. The ownership rights were returned to the family in 2022. Check out the bike path, the Strand, the aquarium and one of the best piers in Southern California. Population: 35,064 (2020).

Manhattan Beach Pier

11.5 *Manhattan Beach, 90266.*

LA River Kayak Safari (LARKS)

11.6 *2825 Benedict St, LA 90039.*

Santa Monica Pier Summer Concert Series - Twilight on the Pier

11.6 Free weekly music festival every Wed, Aug 21-Sept 25, now in it's 35th consecutive year, featuring art, an all new comedy stage, eats, wine and beer garden, games and interactive activations.

Pacific Park

11.7 *380 Santa Monica Pier, Santa Monica 90401.*
Rides, midway games, ocean front specialty food outlets and shopping.

Santa Monica Pier

11.7 *Santa Monica 90401.*

Commerce Casino

11.8 *6121 Telegraph Rd, Commerce 90040.*
Crowne Plaza Hotel.

Hustler Casino

11.8 *1000 W Redondo Beach Blvd, Gardena 90247.*

The Bicycle Hotel & Casino

11.8 *888 Bicycle Casino Dr, Bell Gardens 90201.*

Windsports Hang Gliding

11.8 *12601 Vista Del Mar, Venice, 90293.*
Lessons, advanced soaring, and pilot training at Dockweiler Beach.

Bruce's Beach

11.9 *2600 Highland Ave, Manhattan Beach, 90266.*
Historic site of African American beach resort.

Skirball Cultural Center

11.9 *2701 N Sepulveda Blvd, LA, 90049.*

The Inkwell

12.0 *Santa Monica 90401.*
Site of historic African American beach formerly located near Tower 20 on Santa Monica Beach (at the end of Bay Street). Area is currently called Crescent Bay Park.

LA River Kayaks (LARK)

12.0 *2960 Marsh St, LA 90039.*

Martin Luther King Jr. Hospital

12.0 *1680 E 120th St, LA 90059.*

Original Muscle Beach

12.0 *Ocean Front Walk, Santa Monica 90401.*

Playa Del Rey Beach

12.0 *7313-7351 S Marine Ave, PDR 90293.*

Playa Del Rey Beach

12.0 *7313-7351 S Marine Ave, PDR 90293.*

Santa Monica State Beach

12.0   *Santa Monica 90401.*

Charles Drew University of Medicine and Science

12.1   *1731 E 120th St, LA 90059.*
California's only historically black university.

Autry Museum of the American West

12.1   *4700 Western Heritage Way, LA 90027.*

Gardena Bowling Center

12.2   *15707 Vermont Ave, Gardena, 90247.*
Billiards and arcade also offers a pro shop, lounge & snack bar.

Belvedere Park Lake

12.3   *4914 E 3rd St. East LA 90022.*

Latino Walk of Fame

12.3   *4726 Whittier Blvd, East LA 90022.*

Manhattan Beach Botanical Garden

12.3   *1237 N Peck Ave, Manhattan Beach 90266.*
Located in Polliwog Park.

Alondra Park Lake

12.4   *3850 Manhattan Beach Blvd, Lawndale 90260.*

Watts

12.7   Historic South Central LA community. 90002.

Day of the Drum Festival

12.8   *1727 E. 107th St. LA 90002.*
At Watts Towers. Annually in September.

Simon Rodia Jazz Festival
1727 E. 107th St. LA 90002.
12.8   At Watts Towers. Annually in September.

Watts Towers
1727 E. 107th St. LA 90002.
12.8   Built by Simon Rodia. California Historical Landmark #993.

California State University, Los Angeles
12.9   *LA 90032.*

Compton Creek Natural Park
941 W Cressey St, Compton 90222.
12.9   Featuring natural habitat, walking paths, grassy areas, fitness equipment, picnic areas, amphitheater, parking, plaza, and interpretive signage.

Marsh Street Nature Park
2944 Gleneden St, LA 90039.
12.9   Over 100 trees, native plants, birds, bees and butterflies. Aka, MacAdams Riverfront Park.

Hemingway Park
13.2   *16605 San Pedro St, Carson 90746.*

Marvin Braude Trail
13.3   *15100 Ocean Front Walk, Pacific Palisades, 90272.*

Compton Woodley Airport
901 W Alondra Blvd, Compton 90220.
13.4   Annual aviation fair, flight training, aeronautical museum, helicopter and plane rides.

Old Santa Monica Forestry Station

13.4 *178 Latimer Rd, Santa Monica 90402.*
First experimental forestry station in the US. California
Historic Landmark #840.

Roundhouse Aquarium

13.4 *Manhattan Beach Pier, Manhattan Beach, 90266.*
Free.

Skycap Cafe:

13.4 *901 W Alondra Blvd, Compton 90220.*
Located at Compton-Woodley Airport.

Tomorrow's Aeronautical Museum

13.4 *961 W. Alondra Blvd, Compton 90220.*
At Compton Airport.

Old LA Zoo

13.4 *4801 Griffith Park Dr, LA 90027.*
Founded in 1912, this now-abandoned zoo offers past
enclosure ruins, picnic space & hiking trails.

Bob Baker Marionette Theater

11.4 *4949 York Blvd, LA 90042.*
LA's oldest children's theater company.

De Bell Disc Golf Course

13.5 *1500 E. Walnut Ave., Burbank, 91501.*

Getty Center Central Garden

13.6 *1200 Getty Center Dr, LA 90049.*

LA Zoo & Botanical Gardens

13.6

5333 Zoo Dr, LA 90027.

Home to more than 2,200 mammals, birds, amphibians, and reptiles. The botanical garden features over 800 different plant species.

Thai Town

13.6

Only designated "Thai Town" in the U.S. Try Thai Food and Thai Yoga. At Hollywood Blvd and N Kingley Dr.

The Fran and Ray Stark Sculpture Garden and the Central Garden

13.6

1200 Getty Center Drive, LA 90049.

Bob Baker Marionette Theater

11.4

4949 York Blvd, LA 90042.

LA's oldest children's theater company.

Ferndell Nature Museum

13.7

2800 E Observatory Rd, LA 90027.

Ferndell Nature Preserve

13.7

5375 Red Oak Dr, LA 90068.

Tropical foliage. Man-made brook. 50 fern species.

LA Equestrian Center

13.8

480 Riverside Dr, Burbank 91506.

Horseback riding lessons, trail rides & boarding in a pastoral setting.

Compton

11.8 Known as the Hub City, Compton is home to Compton/ Woodley Airport, Compton College, the Compton Golf Course, the Crystal Casino, the Dominguez Rancho Adobe Museum and Tomorrow's Aeronautical Museum. Compton has served as a creative base for Eazy-E, Ice-Cube, Dr. Dre, Snoop Dogg and Kendrick Lamar and many others. Population: 95,804 (2020).

Debs Lake

13.9 *4235 Monterey Rd, LA 90032.*

Torrance Cultural Arts Center

13.9 *3330 Civic Center Dr, Torrance, CA 90503.*

Will Rogers State Beach

17000 Pacific Coast Hwy, Pacific Palisades, 90272.
13.9 Beach wheelchairs available.

Lynwood Natatorium

3770 MLK Jr. Blvd, Lynwood 90262.
14.0 Olympic size facility.

Redondo Beach

Fifteen parks, recreational harbor, pier and Seaside
14.0 Lagoon. Population: 66,663.

Redondo Beach Fish Market

14.0 *123 Intl. Boardwalk, Redondo Beach 90277.*

Redondo Beach Pier

14.0 *Redondo Beach 90277.*

Compton Library

14.1 *40 W Compton Blvd, Compton 90220.*

Griffith Park & Southern Railroad
14.2 *4400 Crystal Springs Dr, LA 90027.*
Ride one mile course on mini-locomotive.

Hollywood Burbank Airport (BUR)
14.2 *2627 N Hollywood Way, Burbank 91505.*
Only LA airport with direct rail connection to DTLA.

King Harbor Marina
14.4 *208 Yacht Way, Redondo Beach 90277.*

Marvin Braude Bike Trail
14.5 *15100 Ocean Front Walk, Pacific Palisades, 90272.*
Runs from Will Rogers Beach to Torrance.

Compton Past, Present and Future
14.6 *275 N Willowbrook Ave, Compton 90220.*
By Eva Cockcroft. Blue line station.

Griffith Park Merry-Go-Round
14.8 *4730 Crystal Springs Dr, LA 90027.*
Built in 1926, features 68 elaborately decorated horses
& an organ.

Palisades Park Recreation Center
14.8 *851 Alma Real Dr, Pacific Palisades, 90272.*

Dignity Health Sports Park & Tennis Courts
15.0 *18400 S Avalon, Carson 90746.*
Located on the campus of CSUDH.

ZONE FOUR (BLUE PINS): 15.1 MILES TO 30.0 MILES

Dr. Martin Luther King Jr Library
15.1 *17906 S Avalon Blvd, Carson, 90746.*

Storrier Stearns Japanese Garden
15.2 *270 Arlington Dr, Pasadena, CA 91105.*

Blue Line Oasis
1920 S Acacia Ave, Compton 90220.
15.7 By Lynn Aldrich. Blue line station.

Bay Ridge Equestrian
7221 Cortland Ave, Paramount 90723.
15.9 Horse riding school in Paramount, California.

California State University, Dominguez Hills
15.9 *Carson 90747.*

Carson Pool
17.7 *1001 Rose Bowl Dr, Pasadena 91103.*

Tom Mankiewicz Conservation Carousel
16.7 *5333 Zoo Dr, LA 90027.*

Go Kart World
21830 Recreation Rd, Carson 90745.
16.9 Family amusement park. Recreational and competitive driving. All ages and skill levels.

Sky Zone Trampoline Park
1625 W 190th St, Gardena 90248.
16.9   Indoor trampoline park. Freestyle bouncing, dodgeball, and fitness programs.

Dominguez Field and The Famous Titans of Aviation
Atlantic Ave, East Compton 90221.
17.1   By Fausto Fernandez.

East Rancho Dominguez Park Recreation Center
15116 S. Atlantic Ave. Compton, 90221.
17.3   Best known as the park where venus and Serena Williams learned how to play tennis.

Jackie Robinson Statue #2
17.2   *1001 Rose Bowl Dr, Pasadena 91103.*

Travel Town Railroad
5200 Zoo Dr, LA 90027.
17.2   Locomotive museum and mini-train ride.

East Rancho Dominguez Park Recreation Center
15116 S. Atlantic Ave. Compton, 90221.
17.3   Best known as the park where venus and Serena Williams learned how to play tennis.

Jackie and Mack Robinson Memorial
100 Garfield Ave, Pasadena 91101.
17.4   Outdoor sculpture of baseball player Jackie Robinson & his brother, Mack, an Olympic track athlete.

Griffith Park Horse Rentals
1820 Riverside Dr, Glendale 91201.
17.5   Equestrian center offering guided park & mountain trail rides for various ages & levels.

Rose Bowl Stadium

17.7   *1001 Rose Bowl Dr, Pasadena, CA 91103.*

Crystal Casino

17.8   *123 E Artesia Blvd, Compton 90220.*

Compton College

18.0   *1111 E Artesia Blvd, Compton 90221.*

Garden of Flowing Fragrance

18.1   *1151 Oxford Rd, San Marino 91108.*
At the Huntington Library, Art Museum and Botanical Gardens.

Japanese Botanical Garden

18.1   *1151 Oxford Rd, San Marino 91108.*
At the Huntington Library, Art museum and Botanical gardens.

Dominguez Rancho Adobe Museum

18.2   *18127 S. Alameda St, Compton 90220.*

Sepulveda Basin Wildlife Reserve

18.3   *6416 Woodley Ave, Van Nuys 91406.*

Deforest Park Wetlands

19.3   *Long Beach 90805.*
Wildlife habitat, native plants and interpretive signage.

San Gabriel Mission

19.3   *428 S Mission Dr, San Gabriel 91776.*
Founded in 1771.

South Coast Botanic Garden

19.4   *26300 Crenshaw Blvd, Palos Verdes Estates, 90274.*
Koi pond.

📍 **Descanso Botanical Gardens**
19.8 *1418 Descanso Dr, La Cañada Flintridge 91011.*

📍 **Golf N' Stuff**
10555 Firestone Blvd, Norwalk 90650.
19.8 18-hole mini-golf course, arcade, go-karts and rides.

📍 **Long Beach**
20.0 Cool waterfront. Walkable art-filled downtown.

📍 **Dominguez Gap Wetlands**
Long Beach, 90807.
21.4 Urban escape along the LA River with trails for hiking, biking, bird-watching & horseback riding.

📍 **Annia's Kitchen**
4233 Santa Anita Ave, El Monte 91731.
22.0 Home to aircraft and Annia's Kitchen, a casual eatery serving Mexican & American fare in the lobby of the San Gabriel Valley Airport.

📍 **San Gabriel Valley Airport (SGVA)**
4233 Santa Anita Ave, El Monte, CA 91731.
22.0 Home to aircraft, a restaurant, and aviation-related businesses.

📍 **Tropical Foods African Market**
22.7 *4114 Orange Ave, Long Beach 90807.*

📍 **Catalina Express**
Address Here
28.8 A nice way to get to Catalina Island.

📍 **LA World Cruise Center**
100 Swinford St. Wilmington 90744.
22.8 West Coast's largest cruise port.

San Fernando Mission

22.9
15151 San Fernando Mission Blvd, Mission Hills 91345.
Founded on September 8, 1797.

Verdugo Mountains Open Space Preserve

23.0
Oakmount View Dr, Glendale 91209.
Biking & horseback riding.

Los Angeles County Arboretum

23.4 *301 N. Baldwin Ave, Arcadia, 91007.*

Tujunga Ponds Wildlife Sanctuary

21.4 *Sunland-Tujunga, 91040.*

Catalina Express

28.8
Address Here
A nice way to get to Catalina Island.

LA World Cruise Center

22.8
100 Swinford St. Wilmington 90744.
West Coast's largest cruise port.

San Fernando Mission

22.9
15151 San Fernando Mission Blvd, Mission Hills 91345.
Founded on September 8, 1797.

Verdugo Mountains Open Space Preserve

23.0
Oakmount View Dr, Glendale 91209.
Biking & horseback riding.

Los Angeles County Arboretum

23.4 *301 N. Baldwin Ave, Arcadia, 91007.*

Tujunga Ponds Wildlife Sanctuary

21.4 *Sunland-Tujunga, 91040.*

Pio Pico Adobe

23.7 *6003 Pioneer Boulevard, Whittier, 90606.*

Aquarium of the Pacific

24.2 *100 Aquarium Way, Long Beach 90802.*

Museum of Latin American Art Sculpture Garden

24.2 *628 Alamitos Ave, Long Beach 90802.*

Downtown Long Beach Art Walk

24.4 *501 E Broadway, Long Beah 90802.*
Seven city blocks art in 5 galleries, 21 murals, and 30 businesses.

Cerritos Sculpture Garden

25.0 *183rd St, Cerritos 90703.*

Long Beach Airport (LGB)

25.0 *4100 Donald Douglas Dr, Long Beach 90808.*
Serves Long Beach and South Bay.

Pelican Pier Pavillion Arcade and Carousel

25.1 *411 Shoreline Village Drive, Long Beach, 90802.*

Cabrillo Marine Aquarium

25.2 *3720 Stephen M. White Dr, San Pedro 90731.*

The Gardens Casino

25.6 *11871 E Carson St, Hawaiian Gardens 90716.*

Vanalden Cave

25.7 *Vanalden Cave Trail, Tarzana, 91356.*

Santa Anita Park

24.0 *285 W Huntington Dr, Arcadia 91007.*
Live horse racetrack with bars and restaurants.

Earl Burns Miller Japanese Garden
Earl Warren Dr, Long Beach 90840.
27.0   On Cal State Long Beach campus.

Tujunga Ponds Wildlife Sanctuary
21.4   *Sunland-Tujunga, 91040.*

Rancho Los Alamitos Adobe
6400 Bixby Hill Road, Long Beach 90815.
27.3   Built in 1800.

Forrestal Nature Preserve
155-acre, beachfront with hiking trails, picturesque
27.9   lookouts & native animals.

Knott's Berry Farm
28.1   *8039 Beach Blvd, Buena Park 90620.*

Knott's Soak City
8039 Beach Blvd, Buena Park 90620.
28.2   Seasonal water park.

Rio Hondo River
Irwindale 91010.
28.4   An LA River tributary. Starts near Whittier Narrows.

Cave of Munits
24501 Vanowen St, West Hills, 91307.
30.0   Hiking & rock-climbing locale with a series of caves &
elevated sunset views.

Corral Canyon Cave
30.0   *Mesa Peak Motorway, Agoura Hills, CA 91301.*

ZONE FIVE (GREEN PINS): 30.1 MILES AND MORE

Hansen Dam Recreation Center
30.5 *11798 Foothill Blvd, Lake View Terrace 91342.*

Seal Beach National Wildlife Refuge
31.0 *800 Seal Beach Blvd, Seal Beach 90740.*
Encompasses 965 acres.

Zuma Beach
31.8 *30000 Pacific Coast Highway in Malibu.*
Known for its long, wide sands and excellent surf.

Angeles National Forest, Los Angeles River Ranger District Office
32.3 *12371 Little Tujunga Canyon Rd, Sylmar 91342.*
Mountainous national forest covering 700,000-acres with chaparral, pine & fir trees & hiking trails.

California Adventure Park
32.9 *1313 Disneyland Dr, Anaheim 92802.*

Disneyland
32.9 *1313 Disneyland Dr, Anaheim 92802.*

Great Wolf Lodge Water Park
36.3 *12681 Harbor Blvd, Garden Grove 92840.*

San Gabriel River Watershed
39.7 Flows 58 miles southward from the San Gabriel Dam to the Pacific Ocean.

Six Flags Magic Mountain

41.1 *26101 Magic Mountain Pkwy, Valencia 91355*

John Wayne Airport (SNA)

43.3 Serves Orange County.

San Gabriel Mountains National Monument

43.4 *110 N Wabash Ave, Glendora 91741.*

Ontario International Airport (ONT)

Ontario 91761.

47.5 Serves the Inland Empire.

Mt. Baldy Wilderness Preserve

Barrett Stoddard Truck Trail, Claremont 91711.

52.1 Scenic vistas and habitat preservation.

Avalon/Catalina Island

55.0 About 22 miles off-shore. Use the Catalina Express to visit.

Mount Baldy Ski Resort

57.5 *8401 Mt Baldy Rd, Mt Baldy 91759.*

Mountain High Resorts

88.8 *24510 CA-2, Wrightwood, CA 92397.*

Oceanside

Great weather. Gorgeous beaches. Wooden pier. New
90.2 England-style harbor. Check out the Oceanside Sunset
Market every Thursday, it's one of the very best in
Southern California. Population: 175,694.

San Bernardino Mountains

CA 92305.

99.7 The 11,503 foot San Gorgonio Mountain is the tallest
peak in the range.

Snow Summit Mountain Resort

107 *880 Summit Blvd, Big Bear Lake, CA 92315.*

Big Bear Mountain Resort

109 *880 Summit Blvd, Big Bear Lake, CA 92315.*

San Diego

126 Known for its beaches, parks, and warm climate.

Tijuana

142 *Tijuana, Mexico.*
Bustling border town.

Tijuana International Airport

148 Tijuana, Mexico.

Rosarito

156 *Rosarito, Mexico 22710.*
Famous beach town. Check out the Rosarito Beach Hotel.

Ensenada

207 *Mexico, 22800.*
Beach. Harbor. Nice waterfront. Nightlife.

La Bufadora

224 *Mexico, 22800.*
The second largest blowhole in the world, and the only one in North America.

McCarran International Airport (LAS)

272 *5757 Wayne Newton Blvd, Las Vegas, NV 89119.*

INDEX

U

V

W

X

Y

Z

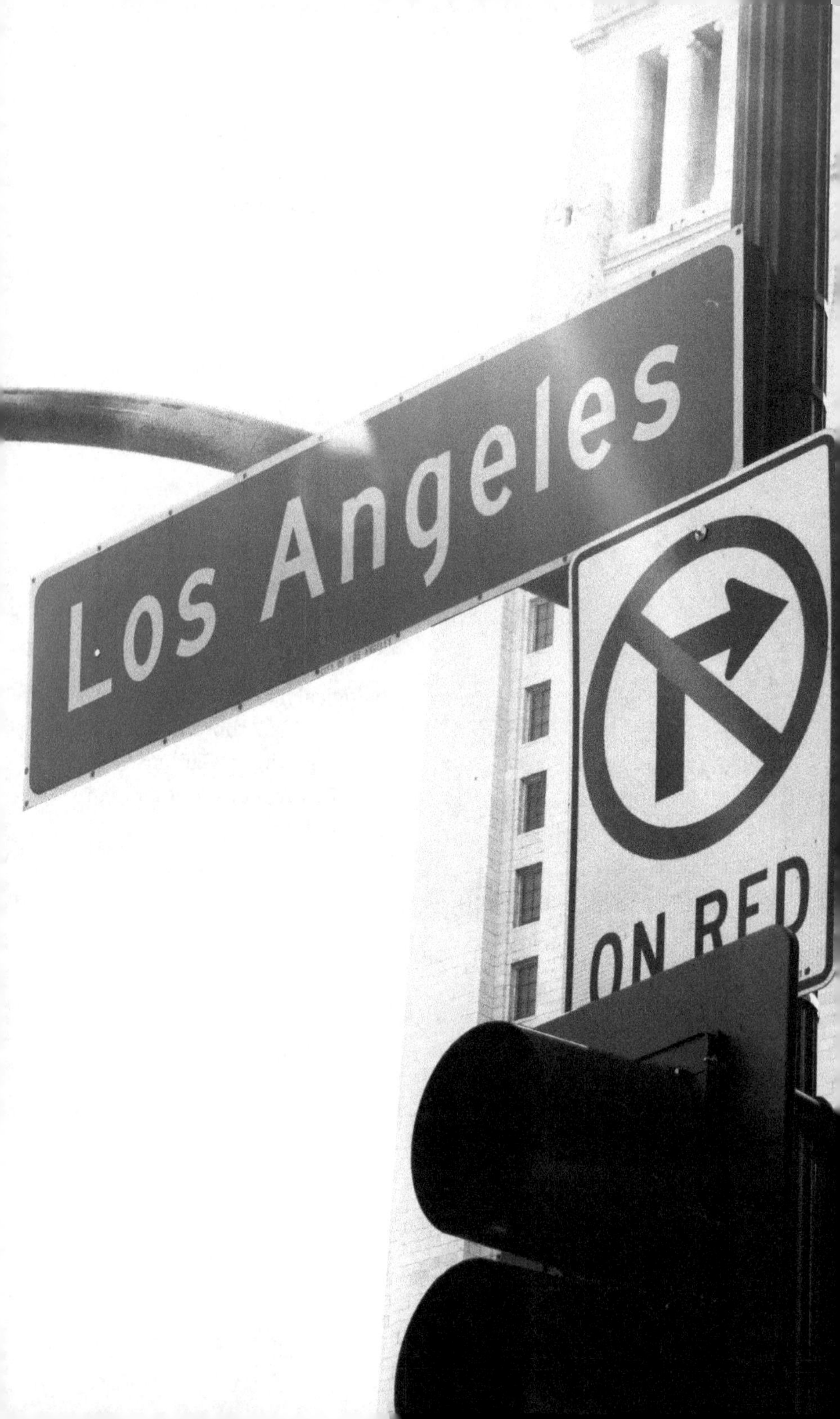
Los Angeles
ON RED

END NOTES

We'd love to know what you think about *Go South LA*. If you purchased the book online, either from a major seller or a small independent, please leave an honest review on your favorite booksellers website.

If you'd like to learn more about things to see, do, hear, taste or experience in South LA, get discounts on cool South LA-oriented gear, or receive Randy's South LA Blog, go to gocrenshaw.com and sign-up for the Go Crenshaw mailing list.

Last, things change so, before venturing out on one of the 700-plus things that you can see, do and experience in and nearby South Los Angeles, we recommend that you:

- Consider your safety by respecting hours of operation, not flashing cash, dressing appropriately for the activities that you are engaged in and by visiting places that are open to the general public, unless you know those places and are known by people there.
- Make sure that businesses (i.e., bars, restaurants, nightclubs, museums, etc) are open.
- Be aware of the best (and the worst) times to go.
- Use the METRO System when it makes sense to do so.
- If you drive, know where you can park your car and how much it will cost.
- Be aware and understand the characteristics of the places you choose to visit.
- Be courteous, smile when appropriate, say hi/ hello, please, thank you and/or excuse me when appropriate.
- Learn something new.
- Do something different than you normally do.
- Enjoy yourself.

ACKNOWLEDGMENTS

I would like to acknowledge the deepest love of my life, my co-time traveler, my one and only wife, Manal Aboelata-Henry for her inspiration, encouragement and support.

I would like to acknowledge my sons, the future of my family, my bridges to the future, Taj and Sadiq for becoming young men with goals, for working towards them, and for bringing me great joy.

I would like to acknowledge my mother, LHM; my father LRH;, my brothers LRHJR, KEH and RAH; and my sisters EMG and GYHW. Y'all know who you are.

ABOUT THE AUTHOR

Randal "Randy" Henry lives in the Crenshaw District with his beloved wife Manal and their two children, Taj, age 18 (freshman at SDSU), and Sadiq (high school junior), age 16, at the time of book publication.

Randy was born and raised in Los Angeles, California. He loves the beach, views of snow-capped mountains, camping trips to Catalina, all kinds of food, whiskey/bourbon, IPA's, skiing, practicing martial arts (capoeira, hapkido and kali/eskrima), Kung Fu movies, family, friends and finding new things to see, do, hear, taste and experience in LA.

Randy has authored numerous scientific articles and several books including *Born in South LA: 100+ Remarkable African Americans Who Were Born, Raised, Lived or Died in South Los Angeles*; *Go Crenshaw: An Afrocentric Guide to the Crenshaw District*; *C is for Capoeira: The Basics of Capoeira From A to Z*; *Black Firsts in Los Angeles, California: 200+ Years of Extraordinary Achievements of Afro-Angelenos*; and the upcoming, *Happened in South LA: An Afrocentric Chronology of 100+ Historic Events that Happened To, In, or Near South Los Angeles, California*. To learn more about Randy's publications, go to www.gocrenshaw.com/author-page.

Randy earned his doctorate and master of public health from UCLA and his BA in Political Science from Cal Poly Pomona. Prior to starting his own firm, Randy worked as a Senior Researcher/Administrator and/or Senior Analyst for the: UCLA School of Medicine; UCLA School of Public Health; Children's Hospital Los Angeles; University of Southern California/Keck School of Medicine; the Los Angeles County Department of Health/Public Health; and, the Veterans Health Administration.

Last, Randy is the Founder of Community Intelligence (CI) Enterprises, an afrocentric health advocacy, education, evaluation, policy and research consulting and book publishing firm.

NOW OPEN

WWW.GOCRENSHAW.SHOP

GOT LOVE FOR CRENSHAW?

Shop the new Black-owned and operated shop
for South LA branded apparel!

BOOKS

TEES

HATS

TOTE BAGS

MUGS & MORE!

#GOCRENSHAW

Scan Me!

WANT TO LEARN MORE ABOUT SOUTH LOS ANGELES?

Visit **www.gocrenshaw.com** to learn more about the neighborhoods of South LA, sign-up for the Go Crenshaw newsletter to stay in-the-know on local events, and find more books about and from the community.

GO CRENSHAW MAPS

Go to **www.gocrenshaw.com** to find maps showcasing things you can see, do, taste or experience in the Crenshaw District.

KEEP IN TOUCH

If you visit any of the places listed in this book, please mention that you read about them in *Go Crenshaw: An Afrocentric Guide to the Crenshaw District.*

 Facebook Group:
Go Crenshaw

 www.gocrenshaw.com

 @gocrenshaw

 www.gocrenshaw.shop

MORE BY THE AUTHOR

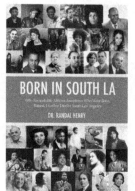

Born in South LA: 100+ Remarkable African Americans Who Were Born, Raised, Lived or Died in South Los Angeles, is a Collective Biography that documents the stories, struggles, accomplishments and events of significance of a few of the amazing people who have contributed to the community known as South Los Angeles.

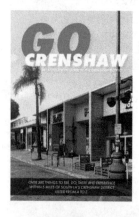

Go Crenshaw: An Afrocentric Guide to the Crenshaw District is the predecessor to *Go South LA* and has 132 distinct categories highlighting over 300 things that you can see, do, taste and experience within 5 miles of the Crenshaw District.

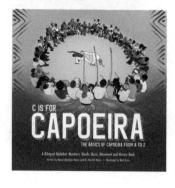

C is for Capoeira: The Basics of Capoeira from A to Z will help you become familiar with capoeira words and sounds and connect them to capoeira movements. More than just a capoeira based alphabet and numbers book, *C is for Capoeira* will make the sounds and sights of capoeira accessible to anyone who is not familiar with them, and engage readers at any stage of life.

PRAISE FOR DR. HENRY'S BOOKS:

"So often it is the narrative of Black failure that dominates the news coming out of South LA. In the popular imagination, this is a place of lawlessness, of poverty, of dysfunction where nothing good happens. *Born in South LA* is a powerful counterargument to this perspective, shining a light on not decades, but centuries of achievement by African Americans despite rampant racism that continues today. [...] This book provides much needed inspiration in a time when we all need more than a little hope!"
— **Karen M.**

"So many times I've struggled with finding places to go and activities for visiting family members to enjoy. It's hard to be a tour guide 'at home'. [...] *Go Crenshaw* is the perfect solution. While it's not exhaustive, as there is so much richness to the Crenshaw District, Leimert Park and surrounding South LA neighborhoods, this guide provides direction that will lead you to well-known points of interest and hidden gems alike."
— **K. Gates**

"*C is for Capoeira* is a beautifully illustrated book that introduces newcomers to everything capoeira, and is sure to inform long-time practitioners too. Most importantly, it does an excellent job of centering the Afro-Brazilian history, experience, and culture as it relates to capoeira and the beautiful art form that was created through my ancestors in Bahia, Brazil. Recommend for all ages!"
— **Mestre Jamaika**

FOLLOW THE AUTHOR

Want to read more of Dr. Henry's work? Follow his Amazon Author Page to always stay up to date on new releases!

Printed in the USA
CPSIA information can be obtained
at www.ICGtesting.com
LVHW010559280823
756437LV00008B/1067